Lost Laws Of Money

Camden Merrik

Table of contents

Introduction: The Money You Were Never Taught

Nobody tells you the score at the beginning of the game. You are handed a uniform, pointed toward the field, and told to run. Work hard. Save what you can. Be responsible. And somewhere out there, the implication goes, a decent life is waiting for you if you just keep your head down and your expenses low.

Most people do exactly that. They work thirty, forty, sometimes fifty years. They clip coupons and forgo vacations and max out their employer match. They do everything they were told. And then, somewhere in their sixties, sitting across from a retirement advisor or opening a statement in a quiet kitchen, the math refuses to cooperate. The number is too small. The years ahead are too many. The window to fix it has narrowed to something that feels almost cruel.

This is not a failure of character. It is not laziness, or lack of ambition, or some personal flaw dressed up as a financial outcome. The uncomfortable truth — the one almost no institution has any incentive to say plainly — is that the majority of people retire broke or close to it not because they did anything wrong, but because they were never taught the rules that actually govern wealth. Not the rules in the pamphlets. The real ones.

There is a body of knowledge about money that once circulated quietly among merchants, landowners, and self-made industrialists across centuries and cultures. Principles about how wealth is created, preserved, and multiplied — not through luck or inheritance, but through a specific way of seeing and making decisions. These were not secrets guarded in smoke-filled rooms. They were simply the common literacy of people who had learned, often through painful trial, what the financial world actually rewards. Over time, as mass education expanded and financial products grew more complex, this literacy was crowded out. What replaced it was a curriculum of compliance: earn, spend moderately, defer to experts, and hope for the best.

The cost of that displacement is not abstract. Run the numbers on a single financial decision made in ignorance at age twenty-five — a choice about debt, or savings, or investment — and compound it across four decades. The gap between knowing and not knowing, between the person who understood the principle and the person who didn't, can easily stretch to hundreds of thousands of dollars. Lifetimes of effort, evaporated. Not to misfortune. To ignorance that was, in many cases, entirely avoidable.

This book calls those missing principles the Lost Laws of wealth.

The research behind them draws from three converging bodies of work. The first is historical: the recorded habits, letters, ledgers, and philosophies of wealth-builders from ancient trading cultures through the industrial age and into the modern era. Stripped of their era-specific details, certain patterns repeat with remarkable consistency. The second is behavioral economics — a field that has spent the last half-century documenting, with rigorous precision, the ways human psychology reliably undermines financial decision-making, and more importantly, how that can be counteracted. The third is observational: the documented behaviors and mindsets of self-made millionaires across wildly different income levels, industries, and countries, people who built lasting financial security not from privilege or genius, but from a particular relationship with money that can be understood and replicated.

If you feel frustrated — if something in you bristles at the idea that you were kept from information that mattered — that frustration is not misplaced. The architecture of mainstream financial education was not designed with your long-term independence as its primary goal. It was designed to produce reliable participants in an economy built on consumption and debt. Knowing that is not a reason for cynicism. It is a reason to get serious.

And getting serious does not require a finance degree, a high salary, a broker, or any special access to Wall Street. Everything in these pages was built to work in ordinary life, with ordinary income, for people who have real bills and real competing demands on their attention. The principles are not complicated. They never were. What they require is understanding, then application, then patience — in that order.

Here is how this book is structured, and why it is built this way. The first section is diagnostic. Before any principle can work, you need to see clearly what is currently working against you — the invisible defaults, the inherited beliefs, the systemic nudges that quietly drain financial momentum. Most people skip this step and wonder why the tactics never stick.

From there, each Lost Law is laid out in sequence. They build on each other. Skipping ahead is possible, but the full picture is the point.

The final section is about synthesis: taking what you have learned and constructing a personal wealth system — not a budget template or a spreadsheet, but a durable framework that runs in the background of your life and compounds over time.

This is not a fast-money book. There are no schemes here, no arbitrage tricks, no promises dressed in enthusiasm. What is here is a permanent shift in how you relate to money — the kind of shift that, once made, you cannot undo and would never want to.

The rules exist. They have always existed.

You just were not told.

Chapter 1 — Why Most People Stay Broke

1.1 The Invisible Architecture of Financial Failure

Do the arithmetic just once and let it land.

The median full-time worker in the United States earns somewhere in the region of fifty thousand dollars a year. Over a forty-year career, that is two million dollars passing through their hands. In Germany, the UK, Canada, Australia — the numbers shift, but the trajectory holds across every developed economy. Ordinary working people do not earn small amounts of money over their lifetimes. They earn fortunes. Small fortunes, yes, but fortunes nonetheless. And yet the Federal Reserve's own data consistently shows that the majority of Americans approaching retirement age have less than a hundred thousand dollars saved. Many have considerably less. A significant portion have nothing at all, or owe more than they own.

Two million dollars in. Near zero out.

Where does it go? The glib answer is expenses — rent, food, the kids, the car. And yes, life costs money. But that answer is too comfortable, because it frames a systemic outcome as a personal one. It suggests the problem is individual spending choices, which conveniently lets every other actor in this story off the hook. The more honest answer is that three distinct forces — none of them accidental, none of them particularly visible — are working in concert to ensure that most of the money most people ever earn flows away from them and toward someone else.

Understanding these forces is not an exercise in victimhood. It is the prerequisite for escaping them.

The first force is a school system that is structurally blind to money.

This is not a complaint about teachers or a nostalgic argument for some golden age of education. It is an observation about design. Modern compulsory education was largely shaped in the nineteenth and early twentieth centuries to produce literate, numerate workers who could follow instructions, meet deadlines, and participate in industrial economies. It did that job well. What it was never asked to do was produce financially independent citizens, because financially independent citizens are, from a certain economic perspective, somewhat inconvenient. They consume less on credit. They are less desperate. They have options.

So the average person graduates after twelve or more years of formal schooling able to analyze literature, apply the quadratic formula, and name the capitals of countries they will never visit — and completely unable to read a loan agreement, understand the difference between an asset and a liability, calculate the real cost of minimum credit card payments, or grasp what compound interest does over time in either direction. These are not advanced concepts. They require no calculus. They are simply never taught.

The consequences are not minor. A person who does not understand compound interest will not feel the urgency of starting to save at twenty-two versus thirty-two. The difference between those two starting points, on a modest monthly contribution at an average market return, can amount to several hundred thousand dollars by retirement. That is not a rounding error. That is the difference between dignity and dependence in old age. And it evaporates quietly, without drama, simply because nobody explained the mechanism during the years when it mattered most.

The second force is a consumer culture that was engineered, deliberately and skillfully, to extract wealth.

This requires some appreciation for scale. The advertising industry alone spends over seven hundred billion dollars globally each year — a figure that dwarfs the GDP of most countries — studying, testing, and refining methods to convert your income into someone else's revenue. Every scroll, every commute, every moment of boredom or insecurity is a surface that has been monetized. This is not paranoia. It is the stated business model, documented in earnings calls and marketing conferences, of some of the largest companies in human history.

The mechanisms are sophisticated. Status anxiety is deliberately stoked because people who feel inadequate spend to compensate. Convenience is weaponized — subscription models, one-click purchasing, and frictionless payment systems are all designed to reduce the psychological resistance between desire and expenditure. Social comparison, once limited to your immediate neighborhood, has been scaled to a global audience via platforms whose revenue depends entirely on how much time and emotional energy you invest in them.

The result is a financial environment in which spending feels natural and effortless while saving feels like deprivation. That feeling is not an accident of human nature. It was manufactured. The average American household carries over ten thousand dollars in credit card debt, paying interest rates that would have been considered predatory by earlier generations. That interest — reliably extracted month after month — represents a direct, ongoing transfer of wealth from households to institutions. The transaction is legal, voluntary in a technical sense, and utterly devastating over time.

The third force is the one people are least willing to examine: inherited belief.

Money is one of the few subjects where emotional inheritance operates almost entirely below the surface. Most people can tell you what their parents believed about politics or religion. Almost nobody can articulate what their parents believed about money — and yet those beliefs, absorbed through decades of overheard conversations, observed behaviors, and offhand comments at kitchen tables, run like background code through virtually every financial decision an adult makes.

In households where money was always scarce, children often internalize the idea that scarcity is the natural state — that wanting more is greedy, that people like us don't get wealthy, that financial security is something that happens to other kinds of people. These are not conscious conclusions. They are emotional weather, absorbed before the critical mind is developed enough to question them. And they express themselves later as self-sabotage: the raise negotiation not attempted, the investment not made because it felt presumptuous, the business idea quietly shelved because deep down the person did not believe they were the type.

Research in behavioral economics — particularly work building on the foundational insights of Kahneman and Tversky, and later extended by scholars like Shlomo Benartzi and Richard Thaler — consistently shows that financial decisions are far more driven by psychological defaults than by rational calculation. Loss aversion, present bias, mental accounting: these are not character flaws. They are predictable cognitive patterns that, left unexamined, produce predictable financial outcomes. And for most people, those patterns were set not by deliberate choice but by the emotional environment of their childhood home.

Taken separately, each of these three forces is significant. Together, they form something close to a trap — an invisible architecture that channels the financial energy of ordinary people away from accumulation and toward expenditure, debt, and eventual depletion. The trap does not announce itself. It feels like life. It feels like how things simply are.

Recognizing it is the first act of breaking out of it.

1.2 — The Scripts Running in the Background

Think about the last time you had a significant sum of money available to you. Maybe it was a tax refund, a bonus, an inheritance, or simply a moment where your account balance was higher than usual. Now think about what happened next — not just what you did, but what you felt. Was there a quiet discomfort? A sudden awareness of things that needed fixing or buying? A vague sense that having that much sitting there was somehow irresponsible, or that it wouldn't last, so you might as well use it?

Most people recognize that feeling. Almost nobody knows where it came from.

The term psychologists and behavioral economists use for this phenomenon is financial programming — the accumulated set of beliefs, emotional associations, and unconscious rules about money that were installed long before you were old enough to evaluate them. The word "programming" is precise, not metaphorical. Just as software determines how a machine responds to inputs, these internal scripts determine how you respond to financial situations — often faster than conscious thought can intervene, and often in ways that directly contradict your stated goals.

The installation happens early and runs deep. Children observe everything. A parent who visibly tenses when bills arrive, who whispers about money as though it were shameful, who responds to any display of affluence with a curled lip and a comment about showing off — that parent is writing code. A household where financial stress is the permanent background radiation of daily life teaches children that money is a source of danger, conflict, and inadequacy. A household where spending is how emotions are managed — where a bad week at work becomes a shopping trip, where celebration means excess — teaches a different lesson, but one equally limiting.

Language is particularly powerful in this process, because phrases heard repeatedly in childhood bypass the analytical mind and settle directly into belief. Consider some of the most common ones. "Money is the root of all evil" — a misquotation, incidentally, of a line from the New Testament that actually refers to the love of money, but rarely quoted with that precision — plants the idea that wealth is morally corrupting, that to pursue it aggressively is to become a worse person. Someone carrying that script will unconsciously self-limit. Every time they approach a threshold that feels like real wealth, the script fires and they find a reason to pull back, overspend, or sabotage the opportunity. The mechanism is invisible. The outcome looks like bad luck.

"Rich people are greedy" does something similar. If you believe that the wealthy acquired what they have through exploitation or moral compromise, then becoming wealthy yourself requires, at some level, becoming someone you despise. The psyche resists this with considerable creativity. "We're not like that" and "we're not a money family" function as identity statements dressed as observations. Money is not just a resource in these frames — it is a signal of character, and the character it signals is not one the speaker admires. Rejecting wealth becomes a form of self-respect.

"You have to work hard for money" sounds positive on its surface — and in moderation, it reflects a real truth. But taken to its logical extreme, it contains a hidden ceiling: money only comes from labor, from physical or mental effort expended in exchange for payment. Someone who deeply holds this belief will find it genuinely uncomfortable, even suspicious, to make money in ways that don't feel like work. Passive income, investment returns, interest — these can trigger a quiet guilt, a sense that the money isn't really earned, which often leads to spending it quickly or dismissing it as insufficient to build on. The script keeps them on the treadmill.

Identifying your own scripts is less about excavating childhood trauma and more about noticing present patterns. Here is a simple diagnostic worth taking seriously. Over the next week, pay attention to three things. First, notice the specific emotions that arise when you check your bank balance, receive an invoice, or are asked to spend or invest money — not the thoughts, but the physical feeling in your body. Second, recall the three to five money-related phrases that were repeated most often in your home growing up. Write them down without editing them. Third, examine the most significant self-defeating financial pattern in your life — debt that keeps recurring, savings that never grow, opportunities consistently passed over — and ask honestly: what would a person have to believe about money to keep producing this outcome?

The answers will not always be comfortable. But they will be informative. And information, in this case, is the beginning of everything.

1.3 — You Were Not Given the Manual

Here is the reframe that changes everything, and it is important to let it settle rather than rush past it: you are not bad with money. The phrase is so commonly deployed — as self-criticism, as resigned explanation, as a kind of personality trait people wear with a mixture of shame and dark humor — that it has come to feel like a diagnosis. It is not. It is a description of an outcome, and outcomes have causes.

A person who cannot perform surgery is not bad at surgery. They were simply never trained. A person who cannot read a blueprint, pilot an aircraft, or write a line of functioning code is not deficient — they were never given the instruction. In virtually every other domain of skill, we accept this logic without hesitation. We understand that competence is downstream of teaching. Nobody apologizes for being unable to do something they were never shown how to do.

Money is the one area where this logic breaks down entirely — where ignorance is treated as a character flaw rather than an educational gap. The person who makes a series of costly financial mistakes is not weak-willed or irresponsible. They are someone who was placed in a sophisticated, high-stakes game without being taught the rules, and then blamed for losing. The fact that nearly everyone is in the same position only makes the individual blame more absurd, not less painful.

The operating manual exists. It always has. It was never distributed — not because the information is impossible to assemble or requires a specialized intellect to absorb, but because the people and institutions best positioned to circulate it had limited incentive to do so. Banks profit from financial confusion. Consumer brands profit from impulsive spending. Predatory lenders profit from people who don't fully understand the instruments they are signing. A financially literate population is, from the perspective of these interests, a less profitable population. This is not conspiracy — it is economics. The incentives are visible to anyone who looks.

What follows in this book is the manual that should have been handed to you before any of it began. Not a summary of conventional financial advice — save more, spend less, diversify — which, while technically accurate, tends to fail in practice because it addresses behavior without addressing the beliefs and frameworks that drive behavior. What follows is a sequence of principles, drawn from the long history of how wealth is actually built, that operate at the level of understanding rather than instruction.

The structure is deliberate. Each principle — each Lost Law — builds on the one before it, because wealth-building is not a collection of unrelated tips. It is a system, and systems require comprehension of how the parts connect before the individual components become useful. A hammer is just a heavy object until you understand what nails are for.

The first section will complete the diagnostic work begun in this chapter — making fully visible the specific mechanisms that have been quietly working against you, so that you can recognize them in real time rather than only in retrospect. The next section introduces each Lost Law in turn, with enough context to make the principle genuinely comprehensible and enough practicality to make it immediately applicable. The final section addresses what most financial books ignore entirely: how to integrate these principles into an actual life, with actual constraints, and build a personal system that runs and compounds over time without requiring heroic willpower or perfect discipline.

There is one mindset shift that makes all of this possible, and it is worth naming plainly before going further. The shift is from "I can't do this" to "I wasn't taught this, but I am learning it now."

Those two statements might appear similar. They are not. The first is a verdict — fixed, absolute, identity-level. The second is a position on a timeline, and timelines move. Everything that follows in these pages assumes you have made that shift, or are willing to make it, because without it the most carefully constructed financial strategy remains just theory. With it, even a modest application of these principles, started late, with limited resources, in imperfect circumstances, can produce outcomes that would have seemed implausible from where you are standing right now.

The rules were always there. You simply weren't shown them.

That changes here.

Chapter 2 — A Brief History of Stolen Wealth Wisdom

2.1 — The Ancient Architecture of Prosperity

Sometime around 1750 BCE, a scribe in the city of Nippur pressed a stylus into wet clay and recorded something that had nothing to do with gods, kings, or military conquest. What he recorded was financial advice. Practical, specific, and eerily familiar financial advice — about saving a portion of every earning before spending anything else, about avoiding debt that carries punishing terms, about making money work by putting it into productive enterprises rather than letting it sit idle. The tablet survived. The civilization that produced it did not. But the principles it contained outlasted everything.

This is the first thing worth understanding about the rules of wealth: they are extraordinarily old. Not old in the way that makes them quaint or historical curiosities, but old in the way that mathematical constants are old — discovered rather than invented, describing something about the structure of reality that does not change because human nature does not change, and because the fundamental mechanics of accumulation are indifferent to the century in which they operate.

Mesopotamia was, among other things, a sophisticated commercial civilization. Babylon in particular developed financial instruments that would be recognizable today — interest-bearing loans, contracts, property records, commodity trading. What the surviving clay tablets reveal is that thoughtful participants in this economy understood, at least intuitively, that wealth was not a matter of earning large sums. It was a matter of managing the relationship between what came in and what went out in a specific, disciplined way. The Code of Hammurabi, often cited for its legal provisions, also contains extensive commercial law — regulations governing lending, wages, and trade that presuppose a population already engaged in complex financial behavior. These were not primitive people guessing at economics. They were practitioners who had refined, through generations of mercantile experience, a working understanding of how wealth accumulates and how it evaporates.

Move forward roughly three thousand years and the geography shifts to the trading cities of Renaissance Italy, but the patterns repeat with a consistency that is difficult to dismiss as coincidence. Florence in the fourteenth and fifteenth centuries was home to something unprecedented in European history: a class of people whose wealth came not from land or noble title but from commerce, banking, and the strategic deployment of capital. The Medici did not become the most powerful family in Europe by accident or inheritance alone. Giovanni di Bicci de' Medici, who founded the family's banking dynasty, operated according to principles that would have been immediately legible to a Babylonian merchant: diversify across ventures, never risk what you cannot afford to lose, reinvest returns before expanding consumption, and cultivate relationships that create financial advantage over time.

The merchant guilds of this period are particularly instructive because they functioned as institutional repositories of financial knowledge. Entry into a guild was not merely professional credentialing — it was access to a body of accumulated commercial wisdom, passed from master to apprentice through observation and deliberate instruction. Apprentices learned not just the technical skills of their trade but the financial principles that separated merchants who built lasting enterprises from those who burned brightly and collapsed. How to price for long-term relationships rather than short-term extraction. How to read a contract for hidden disadvantage. How to reserve against bad seasons. How to think in decades rather than quarters. This knowledge was considered competitive advantage and was guarded accordingly — shared within the guild, withheld from outside it.

The guild system's gradual dissolution over the following centuries did not destroy this knowledge, but it began its long migration away from the common working person. As industrialization concentrated economic power into larger and larger structures, the transmission of financial wisdom became increasingly undemocratic. The principles did not disappear — they continued operating in the hands of those who held them — but the apprenticeship model that had once distributed them broadly collapsed without a replacement.

Cross the Atlantic to the eighteenth and nineteenth centuries, and the pattern appears again in a new context. The early American commercial class — merchants, traders, and industrialists who built fortunes from comparatively modest origins — left behind a documentary record that reveals the same underlying architecture. Benjamin Franklin is the most quoted example, partly because his writing was so direct, but his financial philosophy was not unique to him. It was the common intellectual currency of a certain kind of practical, self-educated commercial mind of his era. Spend less than you earn with enough consistency to make the difference meaningful. Put surplus capital to work rather than storing it inertly. Understand that time is the primary engine of accumulation, and that wasted years cannot be recovered by future intensity.

What is striking about Franklin is not the originality of his thinking but how thoroughly it aligned with principles that had been articulated by Babylonian scribes, Florentine bankers, and Dutch East India Company merchants — people separated from him by thousands of miles and thousands of years. Andrew

Carnegie, whose ascent from impoverished Scottish immigrant to the wealthiest person in the world represents one of the most dramatic wealth-building trajectories in recorded history, operated by a philosophy he was quite explicit about: concentrate resources into the most productive possible use, resist the dispersal of capital into unproductive consumption, and reinvest relentlessly. John D. Rockefeller kept meticulous financial ledgers from the age of sixteen — not because anyone told him to, but because he had arrived intuitively at the understanding that tracking money precisely was the precondition for controlling it. The ledgers survive and reveal a mind already operating, as a teenager, by principles that mirror the Babylonian clay tablets almost exactly.

The consistency across these examples is not accidental and is not romanticized hindsight. It reflects something fundamental about the mechanics of accumulation: there are a limited number of ways that wealth reliably builds, and a limited number of ways it reliably disappears. Human beings across wildly different cultures, eras, and economic contexts have arrived at the same conclusions because the underlying dynamics they were navigating were the same. Money, like water, follows predictable principles of flow. Spend more than you earn consistently and it drains away regardless of how much arrives. Redirect a portion of every inflow before it reaches your spending before it becomes available to disappear, invest that portion into things that generate returns, and leave those returns undisturbed long enough for compounding to begin its geometric work — and wealth accumulates. This is not a theory. It is an observation repeated across millennia.

What changed was not the principles. What changed was who had access to them.

The industrialization of the nineteenth century and the consumer revolution of the twentieth created economic systems of extraordinary complexity — complexity that obscured the underlying mechanics behind layers of products, instruments, and institutions. The person who once learned from a guild master or a merchant parent how money actually worked now received their financial education from advertising, from banks with products to sell, and from a school system with other priorities. The principles did not become less true. They simply became less visible to the people who needed them most.

Understanding that these laws predate capitalism, predate the modern financial system, and predate every contemporary piece of financial advice you have ever received is important for one reason above all others: it removes the excuse of complexity. The rules of wealth are not complicated by nature. They were complicated by design, or at minimum allowed to become complicated without intervention, in ways that served certain interests more than others. Beneath the complexity, the ancient architecture is still standing — exactly where the Babylonian scribes left it, exactly as the Florentine merchants practiced it, exactly as the self-made industrialists of the American century applied it.

The chapters ahead are an excavation of that architecture. Not a history lesson, but a retrieval — pulling these principles out of the past and placing them, whole and functional, into the present where they belong.

2.2 — How the Map Was Taken Away

The disappearance of financial wisdom from everyday life did not happen overnight, and it did not happen by accident. It happened through a sequence of deliberate economic decisions, institutional shifts, and cultural transformations that unfolded across roughly a century — each individually defensible, collectively devastating. To understand how the principles that guided Babylonian merchants and Renaissance bankers vanished from common knowledge, you have to understand what replaced them, and why the replacement was so attractive at the time.

The story has a turning point, and it falls in the early decades of the twentieth century in the United States, though its consequences spread outward to shape consumer culture across the Western world. For most of recorded history, debt carried a social stigma that functioned as a practical restraint. Borrowing was something you did in crisis — a bad harvest, a medical emergency, a business catastrophe — and repaying it as quickly as possible was a matter of personal honor. The notion of taking on debt voluntarily, in advance of need, to purchase things you wanted but could not yet afford, would have struck a medieval merchant or a Victorian shopkeeper as somewhere between reckless and incomprehensible. The word "credit" derives from the Latin credere — to believe, to trust. It was extended by one party to another as an act of measured faith, not as a financial product to be manufactured and sold at scale.

What changed this was a collision between industrial overproduction and commercial ingenuity. By the 1920s, American factories had become dramatically more efficient, producing goods — automobiles, refrigerators, washing machines, radios — faster than the existing population of cash-paying customers could absorb them. The limiting factor on economic growth was no longer supply. It was demand. And demand, several influential business minds realized, could be engineered.

The installment plan had existed in modest forms before, but it was in this period that consumer credit was systematized, normalized, and aggressively marketed as a lifestyle rather than a last resort. General Motors Acceptance Corporation, founded in 1919, was among the earliest large-scale architects of the new model: rather than waiting for customers to save enough to buy a car outright, you sold them the car today and collected the savings — plus interest — over time. The customer got the car immediately. The company got the sale immediately. The bank got a revenue stream. Everyone appeared to win, and in the short term, many did. What the model also did, with quiet efficiency, was begin rewiring the cultural relationship between desire and delay. The ancient principle — defer gratification, accumulate, then spend — was inverted. The new principle was spend now, pay later. The psychological distance between wanting something and having it collapsed, and with it collapsed the saving habit that wealth-building had always depended upon.

The cultural machinery that accelerated this shift was advertising, which underwent its own transformation in the same period. The early advertising industry had largely concerned itself with informing — announcing the existence and features of products to people who might need them. Edward Bernays, Sigmund Freud's nephew and one of the twentieth century's most consequential and least celebrated figures, understood that information alone was a limited commercial tool. What moved people was emotion — specifically, the emotions attached to identity, status, and belonging. By connecting products to psychological needs rather than practical ones, advertising evolved from announcement to manipulation, from description to aspiration. You did not buy a car because you needed transportation. You bought this car because of what it said about who you were. Consumption became the primary language of self-expression, and that language was taught, relentlessly and expensively, to every person who owned a radio, read a magazine, or eventually watched a television.

The simultaneous retreat of financial literacy from formal education was not a conspiracy so much as a deprioritization shaped by economic interest. In the early twentieth century, home economics courses — which included, in many curricula, instruction in household budgeting, debt management, and basic saving principles — were widespread in American and European schools. As the consumer economy expanded and the tax revenues it generated funded public education, the curriculum gradually shifted toward outcomes that served industrial employment: literacy, numeracy, and vocational skills. The nuanced financial reasoning that might lead a student to question whether a purchase made on credit was truly affordable, or to calculate the total cost of a loan against its apparent convenience, was not prioritized. It was not banned. It was simply allowed to wither from neglect.

By the time the credit card arrived in earnest in the late 1950s and 1960s — Diners Club in 1950, BankAmericard, which became Visa, in 1958 — the cultural groundwork had already been thoroughly prepared. A population that had spent two decades purchasing appliances and automobiles on installment plans was not philosophically resistant to a small plastic card that made every purchase equally frictionless. The Diner's Club card was initially positioned as a convenience for businessmen. Within a generation it had become something structurally different: a mechanism for perpetual revolving debt, carrying interest rates that would have been considered criminally usurious in earlier centuries, held by ordinary households as a normal feature of financial life.

What makes this history particularly significant is the profit architecture it created and sustained. Financial illiteracy is not merely a neutral absence of knowledge. It is an active commercial resource. A consumer who does not understand compound interest will not feel the compounding weight of credit card debt accumulating at twenty percent annually. A borrower who cannot read a mortgage document in full comprehension will not identify the clauses that benefit the lender at their expense. A person who has never been taught to distinguish between an asset and a liability will buy things that drain their wealth while believing they are building it. Each of these gaps — educational, conceptual, linguistic — translates directly into revenue for the institutions positioned at the other side of the transaction.

The payday loan industry, which extracts billions annually from people with limited financial options by offering short-term cash at effective annual interest rates that routinely exceed three hundred percent, could not exist in a financially literate population. Neither could the subprime mortgage products that triggered the 2008 financial crisis, sold to borrowers who did not and in many cases could not fully understand what they were signing. These are not fringe phenomena. They are the logical endpoint of a system in which financial knowledge is unevenly distributed and the asymmetry between the knowledgeable party and the uninformed one is both predictable and profitable.

The principles that once moved through guild halls and merchant families and careful parental instruction did not vanish because they stopped working. They vanished because the economic environment evolved in ways that made their absence lucrative for sufficiently powerful interests, and no countervailing institution stepped forward to preserve them.

2.3 — The Laws Were Buried, Not Broken

Everything in the preceding pages has been building toward a single recognition, and it is worth stating without softening it: the financial principles that reliably produce wealth across every era and every culture are not complicated, not new, and not unavailable. They are simply buried — beneath a century of consumer conditioning, beneath financial products engineered to obscure their true costs, beneath an educational silence so complete that most people have never once encountered the foundational ideas that the Medicis operated by, that Franklin articulated, that Carnegie and Rockefeller applied with such deliberate consistency.

Buried is the precise word, because what is buried is not destroyed. It can be excavated. And once retrieved, it functions exactly as it always did, because the underlying mechanics of accumulation do not respond to historical era. They respond to application.

This is the core thesis of everything that follows, and it matters that you understand it as thesis rather than motivation — as a claim about reality rather than an inspirational posture. The laws are not presented here as new discoveries or proprietary frameworks developed in the last decade by someone with a podcast and a personal brand. They are recovered principles, verified across thousands of years of human commercial behavior, translated into language and context appropriate to the life you are actually living. The value is not in their novelty. The value is in their durability.

Consider what that durability actually implies. A financial principle that operated in Babylon, held in Renaissance Florence, was practiced by self-made industrialists in nineteenth-century America, and continues to produce predictable outcomes in the twenty-first century is not a trend. It is not a strategy that worked in a particular interest rate environment and may not survive the next economic cycle. It is something closer to a law of nature — not immutable in the way that physics is immutable, but stable in the way that human psychology is stable, which is to say, stable enough to build a life on.

The implications for how you receive what follows are significant. When a new financial strategy is presented to you — a book that promises the secret to wealth discovered recently, a method developed by someone who cracked a code the world had missed — you are right to approach it with a measure of skepticism. New strategies have a track record measurable in years. The principles in this book have a track record measurable in millennia. That is a different kind of authority, and it should produce a different kind of confidence in the person learning them.

It should also resolve a particular anxiety that plagues people beginning financial change: the fear that they are too late, that the moment for applying these ideas has passed, that the conditions that once made them workable no longer exist. The Babylonian merchant did not have index funds. The Florentine banker did not have a tax-advantaged retirement account. The forms through which the principles express themselves change with the available instruments. The principles themselves do not. If you understand why the principle works, you can translate it into any financial context you inhabit, regardless of its specifics.

What this historical context ultimately provides is not information — though it is that — but permission. Permission to trust what you are about to learn, because it has been trusted and validated by people facing financial realities as demanding and uncertain as your own. Permission to take these ideas seriously, because their longevity is itself a form of proof. And permission to release the self-blame that may have accumulated over years of financial struggle, because you were not failing timeless laws — you were simply never introduced to them.

You have been introduced to them now.

Every law that follows has been here longer than any institution currently holding your debt, managing your account, or selling you a product. Each one was refined through real consequences by real people who needed it to work. Each one is retrievable. Each one is yours.

Chapter 3 — The Law of Financial Identity

3.1 — The Thermostat Nobody Told You About

There is a phenomenon so well-documented and so consistently dramatic that it ought to have permanently changed how we think about the relationship between people and money. It has not, largely because the conclusion it points toward is uncomfortable — not because it implicates the wealthy or the powerful, but because it implicates something far more intimate and therefore far more unsettling. The phenomenon is this: give a person who has never built wealth a very large sum of money, and within a few years, sometimes a few months, that person will find themselves back where they started. The money will be gone, often accompanied by new debts that did not exist before the windfall arrived, and occasionally by a personal life in considerably worse shape than the one the money was supposed to improve.

The lottery data on this is not anecdotal. Researchers examining the financial trajectories of major lottery winners have found, repeatedly, that the majority do not experience the permanent financial transformation you might expect from receiving millions of dollars. A significant proportion end up in financial difficulty within five years. Several studies, including work published in financial economics journals examining Florida lottery winners, found that winning a large sum actually increased the likelihood of bankruptcy within three to five years compared to people who had won smaller amounts. The very size of the windfall — the thing that should have guaranteed security — became a liability.

The instinctive explanation is poor decision-making: they bought too much, gave too much away, trusted the wrong people, failed to get good advice. And while all of these things are frequently true in the details, they describe the surface mechanics rather than the underlying cause. Poor decisions are symptoms. The cause operates one level deeper, in a place that financial advice rarely reaches.

Every person carries what might be called a wealth thermostat — an internal setting that defines, at the level of identity rather than intention, how much money feels normal, manageable, and deserved. Like a thermostat on a wall, it works in both directions. When your financial temperature drops below the set point, forces activate that push it back up — not always consciously, but reliably. You pick up extra work, you cut spending, you find a way. When your financial temperature rises above the set point, equally powerful forces activate in the other direction. Money finds its way out through spending that suddenly seems justified, through generosity that exceeds what you can sustain, through investment decisions that carry risks you would normally never accept, through a creeping organizational chaos in your finances that would, under normal circumstances, have bothered you enough to address.

The lottery winner who goes broke is not a cautionary tale about financial stupidity. They are a precise demonstration of a thermostat returning to its set point. The money was not lost so much as expelled — by a financial identity that had no framework for what seven million dollars was supposed to feel like in the hands of a person like them.

Now consider the opposite case, which is equally instructive and considerably less discussed. There is a well-established pattern among people who have built substantial wealth and then lost it — through bankruptcy, business failure, fraud, or catastrophic personal circumstances — of rebuilding to something close to their original level within a surprisingly short period. This is not universal, but it is common enough to be documentable and too consistent to be random. The rebuilt wealth does not arrive through a stroke of luck or the recovery of lost assets. It arrives through the same mechanisms that built the original wealth — decision patterns, relationship instincts, opportunity recognition, and risk management that apparently survive the loss of everything except the person who possessed them.

The clearest historical examples are businesspeople who entered bankruptcy and returned to prominence. Henry Ford experienced catastrophic financial failure before building the company that bore his name and transformed American industry. Milton Hershey failed twice in the candy business before the circumstances aligned with his capabilities and produced one of the most successful confectionery enterprises in history. These are not stories about resilience in the motivational sense — about picking yourself up and trying again through sheer force of will. They are stories about financial identity that was set high enough to keep generating the behaviors, decisions, and orientations that produce wealth, even after the wealth itself had disappeared. The thermostat was set. The temperature returned.

What determines where the thermostat is set? The answer is the same one that appeared in the previous chapter's examination of financial programming, and the consistency is not coincidental — these ideas connect because they describe the same underlying reality from different angles. The wealth thermostat is calibrated primarily in childhood and early adulthood, through the financial environment you inhabited, the models you observed, the explicit and implicit messages you received about your relationship to money and what you were the kind of person to have. It is reinforced continuously by the social environment you move through as an adult, by the financial norms of your peer group, by the spending and saving patterns that have become habitual enough to feel like personality traits.

The critical insight is that this calibration operates independently of your conscious goals. You can want to be wealthy, sincerely and urgently, and still have a thermostat set to a figure that your behavior will reliably return to, because the thermostat does not respond to desire. It responds to identity — to what feels, at a level beneath rational thought, like the appropriate financial state for a person like you.

This is why information alone almost never produces lasting financial change. People who read about investment strategies and implement them faithfully for a period, then gradually abandon them. People who create budgets that are technically sound and follow them until a stressful month erases the habit. People who receive raises that somehow fail to improve their financial position because expenses expand to meet the new income without any conscious decision being made. In each case, the information was adequate. The intention was genuine. What was missing was an identity that could accommodate and sustain the new behavior. Without that, the thermostat wins every time.

The law of financial identity is the first lost law because it is foundational in the most literal sense: without addressing it, every other principle in this book risks being applied on unstable ground. You can learn the mechanics of wealth-building — and you will, in the chapters ahead — but if your financial identity is set below the level those mechanics are designed to reach, the identity will quietly, persistently undermine the mechanics, and you will find yourself, months or years from now, wondering why the strategies that seemed so clear never quite took hold.

The thermostat, in other words, must be reset before the temperature can change permanently.

3.2 — Resetting the Thermostat

Knowing that a wealth thermostat exists and knowing how to reset it are two different things, and most books that introduce the concept stop somewhere between them — leaving the reader with a vivid diagnosis and no treatment. The framework that follows does not require you to believe in the power of positive thinking or to adopt a philosophy you find intellectually embarrassing. It requires only that you accept what behavioral psychology has established through decades of empirical research: that identity is not fixed, that the brain is more plastic than previously understood, and that the most reliable way to change behavior long-term is to change the self-concept from which behavior naturally flows.

There are three components to resetting the thermostat, and they work best when used together rather than chosen from like items on a menu.

The first is what might be called identity affirmation grounded in evidence — and the grounding is what separates it from the kind of mirror-chanting self-help theater that deserves its skeptical reputation. Conventional affirmations fail for a well-documented reason: when the statement you are repeating is too distant from your current experienced reality, the brain's internal consistency mechanisms register the gap as a lie, and the resulting cognitive dissonance tends to reinforce the original belief rather than replace it. Telling yourself you are a millionaire when your account is overdrawn does not rewire your identity. It produces a quiet internal rejection that hardens the existing self-image.

What works instead is identity affirmation built on actions already taken, however small. The psychologist and habit researcher BJ Fogg, among others, has documented how behavior change is most durable when it reinforces identity rather than merely targeting outcomes. Every time you take an action consistent with a new self-concept, you cast a vote for that identity. The accumulation of those votes, over time, shifts the self-concept in the direction of the behavior rather than waiting for the self-concept to shift before the behavior can begin. In practical terms, this means the statement is not "I am wealthy" but rather "I am someone who makes deliberate financial decisions" — and you say it immediately after you have made one, however modest. Transferred fifty euros to a savings account. Checked your balance without looking away. Declined a purchase you could not genuinely afford. These are identity votes, and they compound exactly as financial returns compound: slowly at first, then with gathering momentum.

The second component is environment design, and it may be the most underestimated lever available for financial identity change. Social psychology has established with considerable consistency that the norms of the groups we inhabit become our norms — not through conscious imitation but through a process so automatic that most people are unaware it is happening. Nicholas Christakis and James Fowler's research into social networks demonstrated that behaviors and even emotional states spread through social connections in ways that are statistically significant up to three degrees of separation. You are influenced not just by the people you know but by the people your people know.

Applied to financial identity, this has a specific and actionable implication: the financial thermostat of the people you spend the most time with is pulling on yours constantly, in whichever direction they are set. If your closest social environment is one in which financial struggle is normalized, in which spending beyond one's means is unremarkable, in which nobody discusses investing or wealth-building because it feels alien to the group's identity, your thermostat will be held at that level by the gravitational pull of belonging. This is not a flaw in your character. It is a predictable consequence of being a social species in which group membership carries survival implications deep enough to override individual intention.

You do not need to abandon existing relationships. You need to deliberately add new ones. Seeking out people who relate to money differently — through professional associations, reading communities, mentorship relationships, or even the careful consumption of content produced by people whose financial identity operates at a higher setting — begins to introduce a competing gravitational pull. The goal is not to become someone else's clone but to expand the range of what feels financially normal and achievable for a person in your world. Environment design is identity design, and it operates whether you are managing it consciously or not.

The third component is future-self journaling, which sounds considerably softer than it is. The technique draws on research into what psychologists call episodic future thinking — the brain's capacity to simulate future experiences with enough vividness that the simulation influences present behavior. Hal Hershfield's work at UCLA demonstrated that people who feel a stronger psychological connection to their future selves make measurably better long-term financial decisions. Brain imaging showed that when participants thought about their future selves, the neural patterns in many cases resembled those activated when thinking about strangers — suggesting a literal psychological disconnect between present self and future self that undermines the motivational logic of long-term planning. When that gap is reduced, behavior changes.

The journaling practice is straightforward but requires consistency to work. Each day, you write in the first person from the perspective of the person you are becoming — not the person you wish you were, but the person who has taken the steps you are currently taking and lived forward from them. You describe not just the financial circumstances of that future self but their relationship with money: how decisions feel, what no longer causes anxiety, what has become automatic that was once difficult. This is not fantasy writing. It is cognitive rehearsal — using the brain's simulation capacity to make the future self vivid enough to influence the present self's choices. The practice, done consistently over weeks rather than days, begins to close the psychological gap that makes long-term sacrifice feel abstract and therefore optional.

3.3 — The 7-Day Identity Challenge

Nothing in the preceding framework produces any result without application, and application requires a starting point specific enough to actually begin. What follows is a seven-day structure designed to do one thing: begin shifting your financial identity before you have changed a single number in your financial life. The order matters. The reflection prompts are not decorative. Each day builds on the one before it, and the cumulative effect at the end of the week is not transformation — that takes longer — but a genuine shift in how you are relating to money, which is the foundation on which everything that follows must be built.

On the first day, the work is diagnostic. Sit with a blank page and write down every belief about money that was present in the home you grew up in — not beliefs you consciously hold now, but the ones that were in the air, expressed in behavior and offhand comments and emotional reactions. Do not filter or evaluate. Write until the page is full. At the bottom, write the answer to this question: which of these beliefs am I still acting on?

On the second day, the work is behavioral. Perform one financial action — any action — that is consistent with a more deliberate financial identity than you currently feel you have. Transfer a small amount to savings. Call to negotiate a bill. Delete a shopping app from your phone. The action is less important than what you do immediately afterward: write a single sentence in the present tense describing who just did that. Not "I am trying to be better with money." Something closer to "I am someone who acts on their financial intentions."

On the third day, the work is environmental. Map your five closest relationships and ask honestly, without judgment, what financial thermostat each of those people appears to operate at. Note where the average of those settings falls. Then identify one person — in your existing network or accessible through deliberate effort — whose financial identity operates at a level you aspire to. Find a way to spend more time with their thinking, whether through direct conversation, their writing, or communities they participate in.

On the fourth day, write your first future-self entry. Set it three years from today. Write for at least fifteen minutes, in first person, present tense, describing your relationship with money in that future moment — not the balance sheet, but the emotional texture. What feels different? What decisions have become easy that once felt impossible? What does financial clarity actually feel like in the body?

On the fifth day, identify the single financial behavior that has most consistently undermined your financial progress — the pattern that has repeated across years regardless of intention. Write a paragraph describing it without self-criticism, the way a scientist would describe a phenomenon they are studying. Then write one sentence identifying the belief about money or about yourself that makes that behavior feel, at some level, appropriate or inevitable.

On the sixth day, return to that belief and write a replacement — not an affirmation in the conventional sense, but a statement grounded in evidence you can actually point to. What have you done, even once, that contradicts the old belief? Build the replacement identity statement from that evidence. Write it on something physical. Put it somewhere you will encounter it without looking for it.

On the seventh day, do nothing new. Review what you have written across the preceding six days without adding to it. Notice what has shifted, even slightly, in how you are thinking about yourself in relation to money. The shift at this point will probably be subtle — a small reduction in the ambient shame many people carry about their financial situation, a slightly more first-person sense of agency rather than victimhood. Write a single paragraph about what you observed.

This is not a program. It is a beginning — a deliberate crack in the financial identity that has been running your decisions without your authorization. Seven days does not reset a thermostat calibrated over decades. What it does is introduce enough dissonance into the existing self-concept to make the new information in the coming chapters land differently than it otherwise would.

The tactics of wealth-building — the budgeting frameworks, the investment principles, the debt elimination strategies — are genuinely powerful. But they are designed to run on a specific operating system, and that operating system is an identity that can hold wealth without immediately finding a reason to expel it. The seven days you just agreed to undertake are the installation of that operating system.

Every law that follows builds on this one. Not chronologically, but structurally — the way a building builds on its foundation, invisibly and permanently, with the foundation doing the work that nothing above it could do without it.

Chapter 4 — The Law of Value Creation

4.1 — The Equation Nobody Taught You

At some point during childhood, most people in the developed world absorb a model of income so simple and so pervasive that it never gets examined. It feels less like an idea and more like a law of nature: you work, you get paid. Specifically, you trade a unit of time — an hour, a shift, a week — for a corresponding unit of money. The more hours you trade, the more money you receive. If you want more money, the logic follows cleanly, you work more hours. The model is clean, intuitive, and for the purpose of generating lasting wealth, almost completely useless.

This is not a criticism of hard work. Hard work, as a character trait, is genuinely valuable — but it is valuable in the way that a powerful engine is valuable, which is to say its value depends entirely on what it is attached to and in which direction it is pointed. An engine of extraordinary power pointed in the wrong direction gets you to the wrong destination faster. Working very hard within the time-for-money model does not escape the model. It optimizes within it, which is a categorically different thing, and the difference matters enormously over the course of a financial life.

The mathematical problem with trading hours for dollars is not subtle once you see it, and once seen, it becomes impossible to unsee. Your time is finite. Every human being alive operates on the same allotment of hours in a day, and the number of those hours available for paid work is constrained by biology, family, health, and the basic requirements of being a person. At some maximum — let's be generous and call it eighty hours a week for a sustained period, which carries its own significant costs — the ceiling on income produced by the time-for-money model becomes visible and fixed. If your hourly rate is thirty dollars, eighty hours produces twenty-four hundred dollars a week. If your hourly rate is three hundred dollars, eighty hours produces twenty-four thousand dollars a week, which is considerably more but still a ceiling, and a ceiling reached only by trading the entirety of your waking life for the currency. Time, once spent, does not return. You cannot save it, bank it, or compound it. The hour worked at twenty-five is gone as completely as the hour worked at sixty-five, and both produced exactly one hour's worth of income.

This is why the time-for-money model cannot, by its mathematical structure, produce wealth. It can produce income. It can produce comfort. In its upper ranges, it can produce a very good life, measured by certain metrics. But wealth — genuine, compounding, self-sustaining financial independence — requires that money continue arriving when your hours are not being sold. And the time-for-money model has no mechanism for that. When the hours stop, the income stops. This is the quiet, unexamined terror beneath the financial anxiety of even high-earning professionals who live well but never feel secure: they know, at some level, that everything depends on continuing to show up, that a sustained illness or an unexpected redundancy or simply the aging of a body that can no longer maintain the pace would expose the fragility of the entire structure.

The Lost Law this chapter introduces is the corrective: income is not determined by time worked but by value delivered. Value, in this context, has a specific meaning that is worth establishing precisely, because the word gets used loosely in ways that drain it of practical usefulness. Value, in the economic sense that determines income, is the measurable improvement in someone else's condition that results from what you provide. The relevant question is never how long something took you to produce. It is what problem it solves, for how many people, and how difficult you are to replace.

These three variables form an equation that explains income more accurately than any other framework available, and more importantly, reveals the specific levers available to anyone who wants to increase what they earn without simply working more hours.

Consider the first variable: the magnitude of the problem solved. An accountant who helps a small business owner save four thousand dollars a year in taxes has solved a meaningful problem. An accountant who restructures the finances of a company facing insolvency and preserves forty million dollars in shareholder value has solved a vastly more significant problem. The technical skills involved may be similar. The training required may have followed the same path. The hours spent may be comparable. But the value delivered is orders of magnitude different, and the income generated reflects that difference, not the hours or even the credentials. The lesson is not that one accountant is more talented or deserving than the other. It is that the market prices problems, not effort.

The second variable — the number of people served — is where the equation begins to separate ordinary income from wealth-generating income in the most dramatic way. A therapist working one-on-one with clients can serve perhaps thirty people per week at maximum capacity. That is a hard ceiling imposed not by skill or dedication but by the format of delivery. The same therapist who writes a book, develops a course, or builds a framework that can be implemented by other practitioners has uncoupled their income from the constraint of personal hours. The value they deliver can now reach hundreds, thousands, or millions of people simultaneously. The income potential scales with the reach, not with the clock. This is not a modern phenomenon created by the internet, though the internet has accelerated it dramatically.

Publishers, inventors, composers, and architects have always understood that a creation, once made, can serve many without requiring its creator to be present for each transaction. The principle is ancient. Only the available tools for implementing it have changed.

The third variable is replacement difficulty — and this is the one that most directly determines whether the value you deliver is compensated generously or merely adequately. Markets pay premiums for scarcity. If what you offer is something that many people can provide to a similar standard, competition drives the price toward its floor regardless of the quality of your specific contribution. If what you offer sits at the intersection of multiple skills, experiences, or perspectives that are individually common but rarely combined, the pool of adequate replacements shrinks dramatically. The surgeon who is also a medical researcher with deep knowledge of a specific rare condition is not simply a better surgeon than average. They occupy a category of one, or close enough to it that the distinction becomes meaningless for pricing purposes. The writer who combines deep technical knowledge of a specialized industry with genuine literary skill and credibility in that industry commands rates that neither the generalist writer nor the industry expert without communication skills can approach. The overlap creates a category, and small categories carry large premiums.

Taken together, the equation reads not as a formula to be calculated but as a lens for examining any income-generating activity. Every time you ask what you should be doing with your working hours, the productive question is not "how can I work more" or even "how can I work more efficiently." The productive questions are: What problem am I solving, and how large is that problem for the person experiencing it? How many people could I solve this problem for, and what is limiting that number? And what would it take to make myself genuinely difficult to replace in this specific work?

These questions are uncomfortable because they require an honest audit of where the work you are currently doing sits within the value equation, and that audit sometimes reveals an answer that is difficult to act on immediately. But the discomfort of seeing clearly is considerably preferable to the alternative: spending decades optimizing within a model that cannot, by its own structure, produce the outcome you are working toward.

The time-for-money model was never designed to make you wealthy. It was designed to make you useful to someone else's wealth-building equation. Understanding the difference is the beginning of writing your own.

4.2 — Three Strategies That Shift the Equation

Understanding that income follows value rather than time is the conceptual breakthrough. What comes next is more practical and, in some ways, more immediately useful: there are specific, learnable strategies for increasing the value you deliver to the marketplace, and none of them require starting from zero, acquiring an advanced degree, or possessing some innate talent that either arrived at birth or didn't. They require honest assessment of what already exists and deliberate decisions about how to position and develop it.

The first strategy is skill stacking, a term that deserves more precise definition than it usually receives. The intuitive version — combine skills to become more valuable — is true but insufficiently specific to act on. The more useful framing is this: in almost every professional field, the people who command the highest compensation are rarely the single most technically accomplished practitioner in that field. They are the people who have added to solid technical competence a set of adjacent capabilities that most technical specialists lack, and that combination creates a category so specific that few people can compete within it.

Scott Adams, the creator of Dilbert, described his own version of this principle in writing about his career: he was not the funniest cartoonist, not the best artist, not the most insightful business critic, but the combination of adequate humor, passable drawing skill, and real corporate experience produced something that effectively had no competition. Each ingredient was ordinary. The combination was not. The principle transfers far beyond cartooning. A nurse who develops genuine expertise in patient communication and conflict resolution is not simply a better nurse — they become a candidate for roles in patient experience, healthcare administration, and medical training that pure clinical skill would never have surfaced. A software developer who can write clearly enough to document complex systems for non-technical audiences, and who understands enough about business to translate technical decisions into commercial implications, occupies a position that neither pure developers nor pure business analysts can fill as effectively. The skills required are not rare individually. Their combination in a single person is.

The practical implication for anyone at any income level is to stop asking "how do I become the best at what I do" and start asking "what second or third capability, added to what I already do well, would create a combination that the market rarely sees and consistently needs." The answer is almost always findable through honest observation of what is missing in your immediate professional environment — the gap between what your field produces abundantly and what it consistently fails to provide.

The second strategy involves solving expensive problems, and it requires a shift in perspective that runs counter to how most people think about the work they are looking for. The conventional job search is organized around roles — titles, responsibilities, industries — rather than around problems. This is understandable but limiting, because it anchors income to what has historically been paid for a category of work rather than to the actual commercial value of the specific problem being addressed. Markets pay for problem elimination in proportion to how much the problem costs when it remains unsolved, which means that identical skills applied to different problems can produce dramatically different income.

A bookkeeper maintaining clean records for a stable small business is solving an administrative problem. A bookkeeper who identifies that a mid-sized company's accounts payable process is generating sixty thousand dollars a year in late fees, duplicate payments, and missed early-payment discounts — and fixes it — is solving a financial hemorrhage. The technical work may overlap substantially. The value delivered is categorically different, and a person who understands this will price and position their work accordingly. The diagnostic question is not "what am I good at" but "where are people or organizations currently losing money, time, or opportunity in ways they can see but haven't solved?" The gap between a recognized problem and an available solution is where value lives, and it is almost always more generously compensated than competent execution of work that everyone already knows how to source.

This applies at every scale. An employee who identifies and solves a problem their employer didn't know to assign becomes indispensable through a different mechanism than an employee who executes assigned work excellently. A freelancer who specializes in a specific, costly problem — website conversion failures, supply chain inefficiencies, regulatory compliance gaps — commands fees that generalist practitioners of the same underlying skill cannot approach. An entrepreneur who builds a business around a problem that costs its sufferers significantly has a pricing floor set by the cost of the problem rather than by competitive market rates for the service.

The third strategy is building assets that deliver value without requiring your direct presence for each delivery, and it is where the equation between the first and second variables — problem size and number of people served — becomes most powerful. An asset, in this context, is anything that continues generating value and therefore income after the initial work of creating it is complete. The obvious examples are financial: investments, rental properties, business equity. But the category extends considerably further and is accessible at income levels where financial asset accumulation is not yet realistic.

A process documented so thoroughly that others can execute it without your oversight is an asset. A reputation built carefully enough in a specific domain that it generates inbound opportunities without active solicitation is an asset. A piece of writing, a course, a framework, a tool — anything that can be used by someone who is not you, at a time when you are not present, to solve a problem they genuinely have — qualifies. The income these assets generate may begin small. The critical difference is structural: unlike hourly income, asset income is not capped by available hours. The work done once can serve many, and the relationship between input and output is no longer linear.

The employee who documents their most valuable processes, the freelancer who packages their methodology into a replicable service, the small business owner who builds systems that allow the business to function without their constant involvement — each is building toward a position where time and income are at least partially decoupled, and where the ceiling imposed by the time-for-money model has been raised or removed.

4.3 — The Audit You Have Been Avoiding

The objection that arrives here is predictable and sincere: this all assumes I have valuable skills to stack, expensive problems I can solve, and assets worth building. What if I genuinely don't? What if the honest answer is that I'm reasonably competent at ordinary things, that nothing I do is particularly special, and that the value equation simply doesn't apply to someone at my level?

This objection deserves a direct response rather than a motivational reframe. The honest answer is that the premise is almost always wrong, but wrong in a specific way: the skills exist, but they are either invisible to the person who holds them, applied in contexts that systematically undervalue them, or never articulated in language that allows the market to recognize and compensate them. Identifying your valuable skills is itself a skill, and most people have never been taught how to perform the audit.

The process begins with a category of ability that is almost universally undercounted: the things you do with ease that others find difficult. This is a more useful starting point than attempting to identify what you are objectively excellent at, because excellence is comparative and often requires external validation that is slow to arrive. What you do with ease that others find difficult is discoverable entirely from your own observation, and it tends to point directly toward genuine differentiated value.

The exercise is structured around three questions, each of which requires genuine time and reflection rather than a quick answer. The first: in the last two years, what have people asked you for help with, repeatedly and from different contexts — work colleagues, friends, family members, people who have just met you? The pattern of requests reveals something about how others perceive your capabilities, which is often more accurate than your own self-assessment. The second question: what activities in your professional life feel almost embarrassingly easy to you, in the sense that you are occasionally surprised when others struggle with them? Ease is not a sign that something lacks value. It is frequently a sign of deep competence so internalized that it has become invisible. The third question: what do you know from experience — lived, professional, or personal — that most people in your immediate environment simply don't have access to? Experience-based knowledge is consistently undervalued as a marketable asset, partly because it was not acquired through formal credentialing and therefore doesn't feel legitimate in the way that a qualification does.

Once these questions have been answered with genuine honesty, the next step is context migration — identifying whether the skills and knowledge surfaced through the audit are being applied in the most valuable context available, or whether they could be repositioned. The same capability can generate dramatically different income depending on who needs it and how urgently. A person with deep experience navigating the disability benefits system, acquired through personal necessity, possesses knowledge that a consultant helping families in that situation could charge significant hourly rates for. A factory supervisor who has spent fifteen years solving logistics problems on a manufacturing floor has operational knowledge that supply chain consulting firms hire for at considerably higher rates than most factory supervisors earn. The knowledge did not change. The context of its application changed the value.

The personal value creation plan that emerges from this audit has three components. First, identify the specific combination of your existing skills and knowledge that creates the most distinctive overlap — your version of the skill stack. Second, identify the most expensive problem in your accessible market that this combination is positioned to address. Third, identify one thing you could create, document, or systematize in the next ninety days that would begin delivering that value without requiring your presence for every instance of delivery.

These are not large steps. They are the right steps taken in the right order, which is an entirely different thing. The insight this chapter is built around — that earning more is a learnable skill rather than a fortunate accident of talent or circumstance — is not motivational rhetoric. It is a description of how the value equation actually operates, verified by the consistent patterns of people who have moved from ordinary income to extraordinary income without extraordinary natural gifts. What they had was a clear understanding of what the market actually pays for, an honest audit of what they could offer within that framework, and the willingness to position themselves accordingly.

The position is available to you. The audit is the beginning.

Chapter 5 — The Law of Retention

5.1 — The Leak Nobody Fixes

There is a line from one of the oldest financial texts ever recovered that has survived roughly four thousand years without requiring revision. It appears in clay tablet records from ancient Babylon, in a passage of financial instruction that translates, with only minor variation depending on the scholar, to something like this: a part of all you earn is yours to keep. Not your landlord's. Not your grocer's. Not the tax collector's, the merchant's, or anyone else's claim on your labor. A portion of every coin that passes through your hands belongs to you permanently, and if you allow all of it to pass through without retaining any, you are not earning — you are merely conducting other people's money from one destination to another, with your effort as the mechanism of transit.

Four thousand years later, the average household in virtually every developed economy is doing exactly that.

This is not hyperbole and it is not a moral judgment. It is an accurate description of the financial structure of most working lives. Income arrives, and then it departs — to housing, to food, to transportation, to debt service, to subscriptions, to the accumulated small expenditures that are individually trivial and collectively consuming. What remains after all of these claims have been satisfied is whatever happens to be left, and whatever happens to be left is what most people treat as their savings. In good months there is something. In difficult months there is nothing, or less than nothing. Over years and decades, the pattern produces a financial position that bears almost no relationship to the total amount earned, because the relationship between earning and retention was never established as a structural priority.

The Babylonian principle — known in contemporary financial writing most commonly as paying yourself first — is the direct and ancient corrective to this pattern. Its mechanics are simple to the point of appearing obvious, which is precisely why it is so consistently underestimated. Before any other financial obligation is met, before the rent, before the utilities, before the groceries and the car payment and the minimum credit card payment, a predetermined percentage of every dollar earned is moved into a separate account that is not accessible for spending. Not whatever is left. Not what seems manageable after everything else has been addressed. The first portion, taken before the spending pattern has any opportunity to absorb it.

The psychological reason this works is rooted in something behavioral economists call the availability effect, which operates on money in essentially the same way it operates on every other resource: what is present and accessible will be used, and what is absent and inaccessible will not be missed with nearly the same intensity. When savings are treated as whatever remains after spending, they are competing against every other financial pressure and desire simultaneously, and they lose that competition with remarkable consistency. When savings are removed before spending begins, they exit the competition entirely. The budget adjusts to what remains, not because discipline has improved but because the psychological baseline has shifted. The money that isn't there cannot be spent, and within a surprisingly short period — usually two to three months — the adjusted spending level begins to feel normal in the way the previous level felt normal, because human beings are considerably more adaptable to constraint than they predict they will be.

The mathematical reason this works is where the argument becomes genuinely difficult to dismiss, even for someone who remains skeptical of the psychological framing. Consider two people who are identical in every financially relevant way: same income, same baseline expenses, same earning trajectory over time, same access to investment opportunities. The single variable between them is retention rate. Person A commits to retaining twenty percent of every dollar earned before any other allocation. Person B retains nothing — not through extravagance necessarily, but through the common pattern of spending to the level of income, meeting obligations, and saving whatever remains, which in practice averages to approximately zero.

At an income of fifty thousand dollars per year, Person A is retaining ten thousand dollars annually. Invested in a diversified index fund at a historically conservative average annual return of seven percent, that ten thousand dollars per year compounds as follows. After ten years, the retained and invested capital has grown to approximately one hundred and thirty-eight thousand dollars. Not from extraordinary income, not from fortunate timing in the market, not from any financial sophistication beyond consistent retention. After twenty-five years, the figure exceeds six hundred and thirty thousand dollars. Person B, having retained nothing across the same period, has a balance that reflects their retention rate: effectively zero in investment assets, plus whatever physical property they may have accumulated and whatever equity they may hold in a home if they purchased one.

The gap between these two people after twenty-five years is not a gap in income. It is not a gap in talent, education, or opportunity. It is a gap produced entirely by one decision, made once and implemented automatically: Person A directed twenty percent of income away from spending before spending could claim it. Everything else in their financial lives was, for the purpose of this illustration, identical.

Six hundred thousand dollars against zero is the cost of not understanding the law of retention. Lived out over a real human life — with the compounding effect of increasing income over time, with the additional returns generated as the investment base grows, with the psychological confidence that accumulated capital produces and the opportunities it makes accessible — the actual divergence between the two trajectories is likely to be considerably larger than this conservative illustration suggests. The number is not the point. The structure is the point. Retention, applied first and applied consistently, is the mechanism by which earned income converts to wealth. Without it, income — regardless of how substantial — circulates through a life without accumulating in it.

This is why the law of retention precedes every conversation about investment strategy, portfolio allocation, tax efficiency, or any other component of sophisticated financial planning. All of those things are meaningful, but they are meaningful only to someone who has something to allocate, position, and protect. The most elegant investment strategy available produces nothing when applied to a retained balance of zero. The Babylonian scribes understood this not as a subtle insight but as the foundational prerequisite — the thing that had to be true before any other financial principle could function. Pay yourself first. A portion of all you earn is yours to keep.

Everything else is downstream of that.

5.2 — The Three-Tier Retention System

The principle established in the previous section is clear enough. What typically fails is not understanding but implementation — the gap between knowing that paying yourself first is the foundational act of wealth-building and actually constructing a system that makes it happen without requiring a daily act of willpower. Willpower is an unreliable financial tool. It depletes under stress, bends under social pressure, and fails with particular reliability at the exact moments when financial discipline matters most. A system built on willpower is a system built on the least stable component available. The solution is to make willpower irrelevant by removing the decision entirely.

Automation is the mechanism, but before automation can be designed, the structure it will serve needs to be clear. The Wealth Retention System operates across three distinct tiers, each serving a specific function in the larger architecture of financial health. They are not interchangeable, and the order in which they are funded matters.

The first tier is the survival account, which is also the most urgently needed and the most consistently neglected. Its function is singular: to absorb financial shocks without requiring debt. An unexpected medical expense, a car repair, a period of reduced income, a household appliance that fails without warning — these are not rare catastrophes. They are ordinary features of financial life that arrive unpredictably and, for anyone without a buffer, trigger a cascade that typically involves high-interest debt, which then consumes future income in debt service, which reduces the money available for the next unexpected expense, which requires more debt. The cycle is self-reinforcing and genuinely difficult to exit once entered. The survival account exists to break the cycle at the entry point, before it begins.

The target for this account is three to six months of essential living expenses — not total spending, but the irreducible minimum required to keep housing, utilities, food, and basic transportation functioning. For most people, this figure is considerably lower than they initially estimate, because it strips out the discretionary spending that feels essential until you examine it carefully. The survival account is held in a savings account that is separate from the account used for daily spending — separate bank if possible, with no attached debit card and no instant transfer capability. The friction of accessing it is a feature, not an inconvenience. It is not an investment account. It does not need to generate significant returns. Its purpose is availability and protection, and those goals are better served by accessibility and stability than by yield.

Until the survival account reaches its target, it receives the majority of whatever is being retained from income. Not forever — just until the buffer is established. This is the one phase of the system where the growth account takes a temporary secondary position, because the mathematical damage done by a single unmanaged financial emergency — the credit card debt accumulated, the investment liquidated at the wrong moment, the compounding disrupted — typically exceeds what modest investment returns could have generated in the same period.

The second tier is the growth account, and this is where the compounding effect demonstrated in the previous section actually lives. Its sole function is to grow. Money that enters this account has one destination: investment. Index funds, retirement accounts, real estate over time, or whatever specific vehicles are appropriate to the individual's circumstances and tax situation. The critical rule of the growth account is that it is not accessible for any purpose other than investment. It is not an emergency fund. It is not a down payment holding area unless the purchase of property is itself an investment by a genuine definition. It is the engine, and engines that are regularly drained for other purposes stop generating power.

The third tier is the freedom account, and its existence is what separates a functional retention system from a miserable one. It is funded from retained income after the survival and growth accounts receive their allocations, and its purpose is guilt-free spending on things that genuinely enrich your life — travel, experiences, quality, generosity, or whatever your specific version of living well actually looks like. The freedom account matters because a retention system that allows for no enjoyment will eventually be abandoned. Human beings are not built for indefinite deprivation in service of abstract future benefit, and any financial plan that ignores this is a plan designed for failure. The freedom account removes the guilt from pleasure spending by making it structural rather than impulsive — money in this account has already cleared its obligations to the future and can be spent without the background anxiety that accompanies spending on credit or at the expense of savings.

The percentage allocation across these three tiers needs to be calibrated to actual income, and the calibration is more flexible than most financial prescriptions allow. The traditional advice — save twenty percent — is genuinely excellent guidance for anyone whose income permits it without causing genuine hardship. But the law of retention does not require twenty percent to function. It requires consistency and automation more than it requires a specific number. An income that makes twenty percent retention immediately viable is relatively uncommon in the early stages of a working life, and telling someone earning thirty thousand dollars a year to retain six thousand before addressing rent and food is not useful advice. It is a formula for abandoning the system within thirty days.

The modified approach for constrained incomes works as follows. Begin with whatever percentage causes no immediate hardship whatsoever — for some people this is five percent, for others it is one percent, and for a small number in genuinely difficult circumstances it may be a fixed amount as small as twenty dollars per paycheck. The specific number matters far less than the structural habit of moving it automatically before spending begins, and far less than the commitment to increase it by one percentage point every time income increases or a recurring expense is eliminated. A person who begins at one percent and increases by one point every six months reaches ten percent retention within five years without ever experiencing a dramatic reduction in available spending. The compounding of the retention rate itself — the habit of incrementally claiming more of your own income — produces a system that accelerates over time rather than plateauing.

Automation is what converts this structure from intention to reality. On the day income arrives — not a few days later, not when convenient — a pre-set automatic transfer moves the designated percentages to the survival account and the growth account. The transfer is scheduled through the bank, not initiated manually each month. It does not require a decision on the day it happens. It simply occurs, the way a utility bill occurs, as a fixed feature of the financial landscape rather than a choice that must be actively made in competition with other choices. What remains in the primary account after the transfers have occurred is the spending budget. Not the starting point of a negotiation between savings and lifestyle — the actual, complete spending budget for the period.

5.3 — The Emotional Case for Keeping Your Money

The practical architecture of the retention system is straightforward enough that most people who encounter it recognize its logic immediately. What stops them from implementing it is rarely confusion about the mechanics. It is something older, more personal, and considerably more resistant to spreadsheet logic: an emotional relationship with spending that the retention system, at first encounter, feels like it is threatening.

The fear of missing out is perhaps the most immediate resistance. It shows up as a specific anxiety — the sense that money moved into accounts that cannot be casually accessed is money that will not be there when something important arrives. A trip that comes together spontaneously. A limited opportunity. An experience that will not repeat. For people who have lived with financial scarcity, the sight of an available balance feels like safety, and the deliberate reduction of that balance — even into accounts that are technically still their own money — triggers something close to panic. The logic of the system says the money is still there. The emotional response says it is gone.

The reframe that actually addresses this, rather than dismissing it, is a shift in what the word available is understood to mean. Money sitting in a spending account is available for everything, which means it has no particular loyalty to the things that matter most. It will go to the spontaneous dinner, the impulsive online purchase, the round of drinks, the upgraded version of something that the standard version would have served perfectly well. Money in a growth account is unavailable for those things and precisely, exclusively available for the thing that actually matters to your future self: freedom. Not the freedom of any single purchase, but the freedom of a life that is not organized around financial necessity — the freedom to choose work rather than being compelled by it, to take risks that constrained finances make impossible, to weather difficulty without it becoming disaster.

Social pressure operates differently and deserves its own treatment. Spending is deeply social in most cultures, and the signals sent by consumption — the car driven, the restaurant chosen, the holiday taken or not taken — carry information about belonging and status that cannot simply be reasoned away. The person who declines to participate in the spending patterns of their peer group is not just making a financial choice. They are potentially signaling difference in ways that have social consequences, and those consequences are real. The appropriate response to this pressure is not to pretend it doesn't exist but to recognize it for what it is: the wealth thermostat of your social environment attempting to regulate yours back toward its setting. The retention system is, among other things, the financial expression of the identity work in the previous chapter — a daily, structural commitment to a financial self-concept that does not require external validation through consumption.

The most philosophically interesting resistance is the belief, genuinely held by many people, that life is short and that deferring gratification indefinitely in service of a future that is not guaranteed is a form of self-betrayal. There is real wisdom somewhere in this objection. A financial plan that requires total present sacrifice for an uncertain future is not a good plan, and the freedom account exists precisely to honor the legitimate claim that the present has on your resources. But the argument that life is short is most commonly deployed not as a philosophical position but as an emotional permission slip for spending that the speaker already knows they will regret. The genuine recognition that time is finite argues not for spending everything now but for allocating resources deliberately — to the present experiences that genuinely enrich life, and to the future freedom that allows the later chapters of a life to be lived on one's own terms. A retained and invested twenty percent does not impoverish the present. It purchases the future.

The retention system can be activated within twenty-four hours of reading this. Open a savings account separate from your primary spending account if you do not already have one — most banks allow this in minutes through an app. Designate it the survival account. Set up an automatic transfer of whatever percentage your honest assessment identifies as sustainable without causing immediate hardship, timed to coincide with each income arrival. Open a second account or confirm the existence of a retirement or investment account for the growth tier. Set a second automatic transfer. Name the freedom account as whatever remains.

The system is now running. Everything from this point is refinement and increase — adjusting percentages as income grows, adding investment sophistication as the growth account accumulates enough to make it worthwhile, building the survival buffer to its target and then redirecting that flow to growth. None of it is complicated. All of it compounds.

A portion of all you earn is yours to keep. The system you have just built is how you keep it.

Chapter 6 — The Law of Compounding Forces

6.1 — The Curve That Breaks People Before It Rewards Them

There is a particular kind of discouragement that visits people who are doing everything right. They have read the books, built the system, made the commitments, and begun the work. Months pass. Sometimes a year passes. They look at where they are and compare it to where they expected to be, and the gap between those two points feels less like a measurement of progress and more like an indictment of the entire endeavor. The savings account exists but holds a modest sum. The new skill is developing but hasn't yet translated into higher income. The reputation being built is real but not yet generating the opportunities it was supposed to generate. Everything is moving, but moving so slowly that the movement is almost indistinguishable from stillness. And so, quietly and with a sense of reasonable pragmatism, they stop.

This is the most expensive moment in a financial life, and it happens to the majority of people who attempt serious wealth-building. Not because they lack commitment or intelligence or genuine desire, but because they stopped at precisely the point where the mathematics of compounding was about to change everything — because they could not see, from inside the early flat portion of the curve, that the steep portion was weeks or months rather than decades away.

Compounding is the most discussed principle in personal finance and simultaneously the least viscerally understood. Everyone who has spent any time with financial education has encountered the graph: a line that begins nearly horizontal, progressing so gradually that early progress is almost invisible, and then at some point bends sharply upward and climbs at a rate that looks, from a distance, almost vertical. The graph is accurate. What it fails to convey is the experience of living inside the early portion of it — the months and years of disciplined action that produce results so modest they feel like evidence of futility rather than evidence of progress. The graph shows the whole curve simultaneously. The person building wealth experiences only the section they are currently in, with no visibility into what comes after the bend.

Albert Einstein may or may not have described compound interest as the eighth wonder of the world — the attribution is disputed among historians, though the sentiment appears in various forms across two centuries of financial writing — but whoever first expressed the idea understood something that most people only grasp in retrospect: the wonder is not in the principle, which is simple enough to explain in a sentence. The wonder is in the numbers that the principle eventually produces, which routinely exceed what human intuition predicts as reasonable.

A single penny doubled every day for thirty days produces a sum exceeding five million dollars. Every person who encounters this for the first time disbelieves it, runs the calculation, and then sits with the result in a moment of genuine cognitive disruption. The mechanism is simple multiplication. The outcome defeats intuition completely. And the reason it defeats intuition is that the human brain, for reasons rooted in evolutionary history, is considerably better at processing linear progressions than exponential ones. We expect results to scale proportionally with time and effort. Compounding does not scale proportionally. It scales geometrically, which means the results in the later periods are not just larger than the early results — they are larger by orders of magnitude that feel almost arbitrary until you have watched them arrive.

But the specific insight this chapter exists to deliver goes considerably further than the familiar compound interest demonstration, because the law of compounding forces is not a principle that applies only to money sitting in an investment account. It is a principle that governs the accumulation of every meaningful resource — and understanding its broader application is what separates people who build wealth from people who build only savings.

Skills compound. This is not a metaphor. It is a description of how expertise actually develops, in a pattern that mirrors the investment curve with uncomfortable precision. The first year of developing any significant skill — a new language, a professional competency, a creative discipline — produces modest, often frustrating results relative to the effort invested. The learning curve is steep and the output is poor. Most people assess the return on their investment of time and energy during this period and conclude, not unreasonably given the evidence available to them, that they are not suited to the thing they are attempting. What they are actually experiencing is the flat portion of the compounding curve. Somewhere between year two and year five, for most skills worth developing, something changes. The foundational competence that was being built through those early frustrating months becomes the substrate on which more sophisticated capability develops, and that capability develops faster than the foundation did, and more sophisticated capability still develops faster than that. The person who committed to a skill for five years is not five times better than the person who committed for one year. They are likely fifty times more capable in practical application, because each layer of competence they built accelerated the acquisition of the next.

Relationships compound in precisely the same way, and this may be the least discussed application of the principle despite being one of the most commercially significant. A professional relationship in its first year is characterized by low trust, limited shared context, and modest mutual value. Two people who do not yet know each other's capabilities, working styles, or reliability cannot collaborate at the level that genuine familiarity enables. Over years of repeated interaction, delivered commitments, and accumulated shared experience, something different develops. The trust becomes dense enough that opportunities are offered before they are announced publicly. Problems are brought for input before formal solutions are sought. Introductions are made because the relationship has generated genuine conviction rather than polite obligation. The network of one person who has maintained fifty deep professional relationships over twenty years generates opportunities of a quality and quantity that bear no comparison to the network of someone with five hundred LinkedIn connections accumulated over the same period without meaningful investment in any of them. The numbers in the address book are not the asset. The compounded trust is the asset.

Reputation compounds, and it does so with a time delay that causes most people to underinvest in it. The actions that build reputation — the consistently excellent work, the delivered promises, the generosity extended without immediate expectation of return, the integrity maintained when no one was watching — produce almost no visible result in the short term. Reputation accrues quietly, invisibly, in the minds of people who are observing your behavior and drawing conclusions they are not yet sharing with you. At some threshold — different for different fields and contexts, but always eventually reached by those who persist — the accumulated reputation reaches a critical mass that begins to generate its own momentum. Opportunities arrive unrequested. Doors open before you knock. The quality of the people who seek you out improves, which improves the quality of the environments you inhabit, which generates further reputation. The compound curve of reputation, once it bends, bends steeply.

The common thread across all of these applications is time, and the common experience of people inside the early phase of any of them is an almost irresistible temptation to redirect their investment elsewhere. When the savings account looks small, the temptation is to stop contributing and use the money for something with a more immediate return. When the skill is developing slowly, the temptation is to pivot to something that seems to offer faster results. When the relationship requires investment without immediate reciprocation, the temptation is to withdraw to a more transactional mode. When the reputation-building work is invisible in its effects, the temptation is to seek more immediately measurable forms of recognition.

Each of these redirections is, from the perspective of the compounding curve, catastrophic — not because the new direction is necessarily wrong, but because it resets the clock. Every time you abandon a compounding investment before the curve bends and begin a new one, you return to the flat portion. A person who has spent fifteen years starting and abandoning various financial and professional compounding investments is not fifteen years along any curve. They are at the beginning of whichever curve they most recently started, with fifteen years of effort behind them and little of the accumulated result that fifteen years of consistent investment in a single direction would have produced.

The people who benefit most visibly from compounding are not those with the highest returns in any given period. They are those who stayed in the game longest without interruption — who endured the flat portion with enough conviction to reach the bend, and then watched the curve do what it was always going to do. The late beneficiaries of compounding are not lucky. They are patient in a way that is only possible when you understand, at a level deeper than intellectual acknowledgment, that the flat portion is not evidence of failure. It is the construction phase of something that will eventually be nearly impossible to stop.

The bend is coming. The only question is whether you will still be invested when it arrives.

6.2 — Building Your First Compounding Engine

The financial industry has a vested interest in making investment appear complicated. This is not a cynical observation — it is a structural reality. An investor who understands clearly what they are doing and why does not need ongoing guidance, does not pay for active management, and does not generate the fee revenue that sustains a significant portion of the advisory business. Complexity is, in this context, a commercial product. It is manufactured and maintained because it creates dependency, and dependency is monetizable in ways that financial clarity is not.

The actual mechanics of building a compounding investment engine for the purpose of long-term wealth accumulation are, stripped of the industry's preferred complexity, straightforward enough to explain completely in the space of a few pages. What follows is that explanation — not a simplified version that omits important details, but the genuine underlying logic that a financially literate person needs to act independently and intelligently.

The foundation of a beginner's compounding engine is index investing, and understanding why requires a brief examination of the alternative. Active fund management — the traditional model in which a professional or team of professionals selects individual stocks or assets with the aim of outperforming the broader market — sounds intuitively superior to simply buying the whole market and accepting whatever return it generates. Skilled people, applying sophisticated analysis, should logically do better than an undiscriminating approach that owns everything indiscriminately. The data, accumulated over decades and across markets, consistently fails to support this intuition. The majority of actively managed funds underperform their relevant index over periods of ten years or longer, and the minority that do outperform in any given period show little consistency in maintaining that outperformance in subsequent periods. The reason is partly the genuine difficulty of consistently predicting market behavior, and partly arithmetic: active management costs money in the form of management fees, transaction costs, and tax consequences of frequent trading, and those costs must be overcome before any outperformance can benefit the investor. An index fund that simply holds the components of a market index — the S&P 500, a total world market index, or a bond index — carries costs that are a fraction of those associated with active management, and those lower costs compound over time just as returns do, but in the investor's favor rather than the manager's.

A practical starting engine for someone beginning from zero consists of two or three index funds held in a tax-advantaged account where one is available. In the United States, this means a Roth IRA or a 401k. In the United Kingdom, an ISA. In most European countries, pension wrappers or their local equivalent exist that reduce or eliminate the tax drag on investment returns. The specific account type matters because the compounding curve is significantly steeper inside a tax-advantaged account than outside one — every dollar that would have left as tax instead remains invested, generating returns, generating returns on those returns, for the full duration of the investment period. Using taxable accounts when tax-advantaged options are available and unfilled is one of the most common and costly mistakes beginning investors make, usually through simple unawareness that the option exists.

The fund selection, inside a tax-advantaged account, can reasonably consist of a total stock market index fund, a total international stock market index fund, and a bond index fund, with the allocation between them reflecting the investor's time horizon. Someone with thirty or more years before they will need the money can hold a portfolio weighted heavily toward equities — eighty to ninety percent — because the historical behavior of equity markets over long periods shows that short-term volatility, which is the actual risk being managed, becomes progressively less consequential as the time horizon extends. Someone within ten years of needing the money introduces more bonds to reduce the exposure to a badly timed market downturn immediately before withdrawal. These are not sophisticated decisions requiring professional guidance. They are reasonable responses to mathematical realities about time and risk that any attentive person can understand and apply.

The mathematics of starting early versus starting with more money resolves clearly in favor of time, and the resolution is dramatic enough to be worth examining with actual numbers rather than abstract principle. An investor who begins at twenty-five, contributes three hundred dollars per month to an index fund earning an average of seven percent annually, and continues until sixty-five will accumulate approximately eight hundred thousand dollars. An investor who waits until thirty-five to begin, then contributes six hundred dollars per month — double the amount — for the same thirty-year period at the same return will accumulate approximately seven hundred and fifty thousand dollars. The person who started earlier, contributing half as much money per month, ends with more. The difference is entirely attributable to the additional decade at the beginning, during which the contributions had the most time to compound. The implication is significant: the optimal moment to begin is always as early as possible, and the second-best moment is immediately, because every additional month at the beginning of the curve is worth considerably more than any equivalent month later.

The one-hour-per-week investment management system is not a regimented program so much as a description of what genuinely good long-term index investing actually requires in practice. Once the accounts are open, the funds are selected, and the automatic contributions are running — which are the tasks that require the most initial attention and perhaps a few hours of focused effort to establish — the ongoing maintenance of a long-term index portfolio is minimal by design. One hour per week is, if anything, generous. The tasks are few: confirming that automatic contributions are executing as planned, conducting a quarterly review of whether the allocation between equities and bonds still reflects your intended risk level, rebalancing annually if the market's movements have shifted the allocation meaningfully away from the target, and reading enough to stay informed about any significant changes to the accounts or funds without consuming so much financial media that emotional reactions to short-term market movements begin to influence long-term decisions.

That last point deserves emphasis. The primary risk to a long-term index investor is not market volatility. It is their own behavioral response to market volatility — the impulse to sell when markets fall sharply, which converts a temporary paper loss into a permanent realized one and removes capital from the market during the period when it historically offers the best forward returns. Limiting financial media consumption to what is necessary for genuine decision-making is therefore not laziness. It is a protective strategy against the most statistically dangerous behavior available to a long-term investor.

6.3 — The Enemies of Compounding

A compounding engine running without protection is an engine with holes in it. The returns generated on one side are being drained from the other, and if the drains are large enough or numerous enough, the engine that appeared to be accumulating wealth is, net of its losses, doing considerably less than the raw return numbers suggest. There are four primary enemies of compounding, each operating through a different mechanism, each addressable through specific countermeasures that are well within the capability of any financially attentive person.

Inflation is the most insidious of the four because it operates invisibly and because its effects are felt in the future rather than the present, making them easy to discount. At a sustained inflation rate of three percent annually, the purchasing power of a sum of money held in a non-interest-bearing account halves in roughly twenty-four years. This means that saving money in a form that earns less than the inflation rate — a standard checking account, cash under the proverbial mattress, or any vehicle returning less than three percent — is not a neutral act. It is a slow, guaranteed loss of real value. The countermeasure is ensuring that retained capital is always working at a return that exceeds the inflation rate by a meaningful margin, which historically index investing in equities has achieved over long periods, and which at minimum requires that cash savings beyond the emergency buffer be held in a high-yield savings account rather than a standard one. The gap between what a standard savings account pays and what a high-yield equivalent pays on the same balance compounds over years into a meaningful difference in purchasing power.

Fees are the compounding enemy that the financial industry would prefer you not examine too carefully. The reason is that fees compound in exactly the same way returns do — they are a percentage of the total invested, applied annually, which means they grow as the portfolio grows and drain an increasing absolute amount as the portfolio increases in size. The difference between an expense ratio of one percent and an expense ratio of zero point one percent — the approximate difference between an actively managed fund and a comparable index fund — appears trivially small in year one. On a portfolio of five hundred thousand dollars over twenty years, assuming equivalent gross returns, the difference in cumulative fees exceeds one hundred and fifty thousand dollars. The countermeasure is straightforward: minimize fees everywhere they exist. Choose index funds over actively managed funds. Choose the lower-cost share class when multiple options exist for the same fund. Avoid products that carry front-end or back-end sales loads. Review account fees annually and consolidate accounts where doing so reduces costs.

Taxes represent the third compounding drain and the one over which an informed investor has the most direct control. Investment returns generated inside a tax-advantaged account compound without interruption. The same returns generated in a taxable account are reduced by tax at each realization event — each sale, each dividend, each distribution — and the after-tax amount is what compounds forward. Over decades, the difference between the two environments is substantial, which is why maximizing contributions to tax-advantaged accounts before investing in taxable accounts is the first and most powerful tax countermeasure available. Within taxable accounts, holding investments for longer than one year before selling converts gains from ordinary income tax rates to the lower long-term capital gains rates in most jurisdictions. Tax-loss harvesting — selling positions that have declined in value to realize a loss that offsets gains elsewhere — is a further technique that becomes worth implementing as the portfolio grows to a size that makes the effort worthwhile.

Lifestyle creep is perhaps the most personally threatening of the four enemies because it arrives disguised as a reward. Every income increase creates a new margin between what was previously earned and what is now earned, and that margin feels like permission to improve the quality of daily life — a nicer apartment, a better car, more frequent dining out, upgraded travel. Each individual upgrade is reasonable and enjoyable. Their cumulative effect, if the majority of every income increase is absorbed by lifestyle rather than directed to the growth account, is the perpetual maintenance of a gap between income and retention that never narrows regardless of how much earning increases. The person who earns fifty thousand and saves ten thousand is in the same proportional position as the person who earns a hundred and fifty thousand and saves thirty thousand, but no better than the person who earns a hundred and fifty thousand and saves ten — which is the actual outcome of unchecked lifestyle creep applied across a career of increasing income.

The countermeasure is a commitment made in advance rather than in the moment of receiving good news: when income increases, direct a predetermined percentage of the increase — at minimum fifty percent, ideally more — to the growth account before adjusting lifestyle spending. The lifestyle improvement then comes from what remains after that commitment is honored, which still represents real improvement in daily quality of life while simultaneously accelerating the compounding engine. This agreement with your future self, made during a calm moment of planning rather than in the glow of a raise or a windfall, is one of the most high-leverage financial decisions available at any income level.

With the engine running and the four shields in place, compounding does what it has always done: it works. Quietly, persistently, and with increasing force as time accumulates. The flat portion of the curve, endured with understanding rather than abandoned in frustration, eventually becomes the steep portion. The steep portion, protected from the enemies that would drain it, becomes the financial independence that the Babylonian scribes were pointing toward four thousand years ago when they said, with a simplicity that has never been improved upon, that a part of all you earn is yours to keep.

Chapter 7 — The Law of Strategic Debt

7.1 — The Tool That Works Both Ways

Pick up a scalpel and you can save a life or end one. The instrument itself carries no moral charge. What determines the outcome is the knowledge, intention, and skill of the person holding it. Debt works by precisely the same logic, and the failure to understand this — the cultural habit of treating debt as uniformly shameful or uniformly acceptable depending on which oversimplification your upbringing favored — is responsible for two equally damaging errors. The first error is using destructive debt casually and chronically, draining wealth through a thousand small cuts of interest paid on things already consumed. The second error is avoiding all debt categorically, including the forms that the wealthiest and most financially sophisticated individuals and institutions on earth use deliberately and systematically to build assets they could never have acquired with cash alone.

Both errors keep people poor. They do so through opposite mechanisms, but the destination is the same: a financial life in which debt is either a slow hemorrhage or a missed instrument, and in neither case a tool being wielded intelligently toward a defined purpose.

The distinction that resolves this confusion is not complicated, but it requires precision to be genuinely useful rather than merely conceptually satisfying. Destructive debt is money borrowed to fund consumption — to purchase things that depreciate in value, generate no return, and leave the borrower with a liability on their balance sheet and nothing productive on the asset side. A credit card balance carried month to month on restaurant meals, clothing, electronics, and daily expenses is the clearest example. The meal was consumed. The clothing is depreciating in both condition and resale value. The electronics will be obsolete within years. None of it generates income. None of it appreciates. What remains is the debt — and attached to that debt, at rates that in many cases exceed twenty percent annually, is a compounding interest charge that is building wealth for the lender with the same mathematical force that the previous chapter showed building wealth for the investor. The borrower is on the wrong side of that equation. They are the engine of someone else's compounding.

Car loans sit in similar territory for most buyers, though the analysis requires a moment of honest examination. The vehicle purchased on credit is a depreciating asset — it loses value from the moment it leaves the lot, reliably and substantially, regardless of how well it is maintained. The loan attached to it carries an interest rate that adds meaningfully to its total cost. The combination means the buyer is paying more than the purchase price for something worth progressively less than what they paid. For a vehicle that is genuinely necessary for income generation — a tradesperson's work van, a delivery driver's car — the analysis shifts, because the asset is now generating returns that can be set against its cost. For the vast majority of consumer vehicle purchases, no such returns exist. The car is a consumption item financed over time, and the financing makes it more expensive without making it more productive.

Consumer personal loans, buy-now-pay-later schemes, and the accumulated small debt instruments that have proliferated across the digital economy in the last decade operate by identical logic. They move consumption forward in time, allow immediate access to things the borrower has not yet earned the money to purchase, and extract a price for that convenience in the form of interest that compounds in the lender's favor. The convenience is real. The cost, when examined across the full term and total interest paid rather than merely the monthly payment, is almost always substantially higher than the borrower intuitively appreciates at the point of taking it on.

This is the debt that has trapped millions of people in a cycle that is genuinely difficult to exit once established. It is not that individual pieces of consumer debt are catastrophic in isolation. A single credit card balance of two thousand dollars, while not ideal, is a manageable problem. The trap is structural: consumer debt tends to accumulate gradually and across multiple instruments simultaneously, reaching a combined monthly service cost that consumes a significant percentage of income and leaves insufficient margin to build the retained capital that would allow the debt to be eliminated. The income goes to debt service. The absence of retained capital means any unexpected expense requires more debt. The new debt increases the service cost. The increased service cost reduces the margin further. The cycle turns, and the financial position deteriorates not through any single dramatic event but through the quiet, monthly arithmetic of interest paid on consumption already gone.

Strategic debt is a categorically different instrument despite sharing the same fundamental mechanism — money borrowed at a cost, to be repaid over time. What makes it strategic is that it is deployed to acquire assets that generate returns exceeding the cost of the borrowing, which means the debt is effectively paying for itself while simultaneously building the borrower's net worth in a way that would have been impossible or significantly slower without leverage.

Real estate is the most accessible and historically consistent example of strategic debt in practice, and examining its mechanics precisely — rather than in the vague inspirational terms that populate most real estate investment content — reveals why the wealthy have used property leverage as a wealth-building instrument across virtually every era and culture for which financial records exist. A property purchased for three hundred thousand dollars with a twenty percent down payment of sixty thousand dollars uses sixty thousand dollars of the buyer's capital to control an asset worth three hundred thousand dollars. If that property appreciates at four percent annually — a conservative estimate across most developed market property over long periods — the appreciation in year one is twelve thousand dollars, generated on a sixty-thousand-dollar cash investment. That is a twenty percent return on the actual capital deployed, achieved through an asset that returned only four percent on its total value. The leverage multiplied the return. Additionally, if the property generates rental income that covers the mortgage payment and carrying costs, the asset is servicing its own debt while appreciating. The debt is not a drain in this structure. It is the mechanism by which a relatively modest capital outlay controls and benefits from a substantially larger asset.

Business debt operates by similar logic when deployed deliberately. A business owner who borrows to purchase equipment that increases productive capacity, to fund inventory for a contracted order that will generate profit exceeding the financing cost, or to acquire a competitor whose integration will produce returns above the cost of acquisition is using debt as a multiplier of productive capacity. The debt is not consumption. It is investment, and the returns on that investment, if the analysis is honest and the execution competent, justify and service the borrowing from the income the borrowed capital helped generate.

The wealthy understand this distinction not as a theoretical framework but as operational practice. Major corporations carry debt deliberately and strategically, maintaining capital structures that use borrowed money at relatively low interest rates to fund operations and acquisitions that generate returns significantly above those rates. Real estate investors use mortgage leverage to control portfolios worth multiples of their actual invested capital. Private equity firms build their entire business model around the intelligent deployment of leveraged capital into productive assets. None of these actors are confused about debt. They have simply learned to read the instrument precisely — to distinguish the cost of the borrowing from the return on what it purchased, and to proceed only when the return demonstrably exceeds the cost by a margin that justifies the risk.

The person who has been taught only that debt is bad, or only that debt is normal and unavoidable, has been handed an incomplete map of the territory. The complete map shows two very different landscapes: one in which debt extracts wealth through consumption financing, and one in which debt amplifies wealth through asset acquisition. The geography of these two landscapes is not always immediately obvious — some instruments present themselves as one thing while functioning as another — but the test is always the same. Does this borrowed money acquire something that generates returns? Will those returns exceed the cost of the borrowing over the relevant period? Does the asset side of the resulting balance sheet grow faster than the liability? If the answers are yes, yes, and yes, the debt may be strategic. If any answer is no, the debt is likely destructive regardless of how it is marketed or how reasonable the monthly payment appears.

The scalpel, understood and used correctly, is among the most powerful tools in a surgeon's hands. Misunderstood or misused, it causes the damage it was designed to prevent. The law of strategic debt is the operating manual for the financial instrument that most people handle without ever having read it.

7.2 — The Cascade Method: Eliminating Destructive Debt

Getting out of destructive debt is not primarily a mathematical problem. If it were, the solution would be obvious to anyone with access to a calculator, and the debt would resolve itself through simple application of arithmetic. The reason debt elimination fails so consistently — the reason people begin plans with genuine commitment and abandon them six months later, the reason the same balances reappear on the same cards year after year despite sincere efforts to eliminate them — is that debt elimination is primarily a psychological problem that also requires correct mathematics. A method that optimizes only for math will fail for psychological reasons. A method that optimizes only for motivation will fail because the numbers are wrong. The cascade method addresses both simultaneously, which is why it outperforms either approach used alone.

The first step is a complete inventory, conducted once, without flinching. Every debt instrument you carry — credit cards, personal loans, car loans, student loans, buy-now-pay-later balances, money owed to family members, everything — goes onto a single page with four pieces of information beside each entry: the current outstanding balance, the interest rate being charged, the minimum monthly payment required, and the total monthly interest cost in actual dollars. That last figure is the one most people have never calculated and find most clarifying. An interest rate of twenty-two percent on a four-thousand-dollar balance is not an abstract percentage. It is seventy-three dollars leaving your account every single month in exchange for nothing — no product, no service, no asset, no experience. It is pure extraction, paid for the privilege of having borrowed money that in many cases purchased things no longer in your possession. Seeing the monthly interest cost in dollars rather than percentages changes the emotional register of the debt in a way that motivates action more effectively than any abstract awareness of the rate.

Once the inventory is complete, the cascade method sequences the elimination in a specific order that combines mathematical efficiency with psychological sustainability. List all debts from the highest interest rate to the lowest. The highest-rate debt is the one extracting the most wealth from you per dollar of outstanding balance, which makes it the most urgent by any rational financial measure. This is the debt that receives every available dollar above the minimum payments on all other debts. The minimum payments on everything else are maintained without exception — missed minimums trigger fees and credit score damage that create new problems — but any margin between your total income and your total essential expenses plus minimum payments is directed entirely to the highest-rate debt until it is gone.

When the highest-rate debt reaches zero, the payment that had been going to it does not return to general spending. It cascades — the full amount, minimum and surplus together, redirects to the next debt on the list. The elimination of each successive debt accelerates because the payment available to attack it is larger than the one that attacked the previous debt. The cascade builds momentum in both the mathematical and psychological sense, and the psychological dimension matters because debt elimination is a long-horizon commitment that requires sustained motivation. Each eliminated debt is a concrete, complete victory — a creditor permanently removed from your financial life, a monthly obligation that no longer exists, a small but real increase in the margin available for the next target.

The worksheet that makes this operational is straightforward. Column one lists the creditor. Column two lists the balance. Column three lists the rate. Column four lists the minimum payment. Column five lists the monthly interest cost in dollars. At the bottom, total the minimum payments and subtract from the monthly margin available for debt elimination. The surplus, however large or small, goes entirely to the top item on the list. The list is reviewed monthly, updated as balances change, and reordered if rates change. Nothing else requires attention except maintaining the minimums and directing the surplus consistently.

Before implementing the cascade, there is a step that many people skip because it feels uncomfortable and that consistently proves worthwhile: negotiating the rates themselves. Credit card companies in particular have considerably more flexibility on interest rates than they advertise, and a direct phone call requesting a rate reduction succeeds more often than most cardholders expect. The conversation requires neither aggression nor elaborate justification. A version of the following tends to work: you have been a customer for a number of years and have generally maintained your account responsibly. You are aware that your current rate is significantly above what competitors are currently offering for balance transfers, and you would prefer to keep the account rather than transfer the balance, but you would need a rate reduction to make that viable. You are asking whether they are able to accommodate that. The worst outcome of this call is the same rate you started with. The best outcome, which occurs in a meaningful proportion of cases, is an immediate reduction of several percentage points that reduces the monthly interest cost and accelerates the elimination timeline without any additional payment required.

For accounts where the balance has been in difficulty and settlement is a possibility, the conversation shifts. Credit card companies regularly settle delinquent balances for between forty and sixty cents on the dollar when they assess the alternative as prolonged non-payment or charge-off. A settlement call should begin with an honest acknowledgment of the account's status, a statement that you are attempting to resolve the balance and have access to a lump sum, and a specific offer below the outstanding balance. Get any agreed settlement in writing before transferring any funds, confirm that the agreement specifies the account will be reported as settled to the credit bureaus, and retain the written confirmation permanently. The credit impact of a settled account is real but temporary and considerably less damaging than the ongoing financial impact of carrying the full balance at full interest indefinitely.

7.3 — Using Debt as a Wealth Instrument

The transition from debt elimination to strategic debt deployment is not a simultaneous move. It is a sequential one, and the sequencing is important. The guardrails that prevent catastrophic mistakes with leveraged capital begin with the prerequisite that destructive debt is eliminated or substantially controlled before borrowed money is used to pursue assets. The reason is structural rather than moralistic: a person carrying high-interest consumer debt while simultaneously taking on investment debt is paying a guaranteed high cost on one side while pursuing an uncertain return on the other, and the net position is frequently worse than either situation alone. Eliminate the drain before opening the tap.

When the position is clean enough to consider strategic deployment, the principles that separate intelligent leverage from dangerous speculation reduce to a handful of tests that should be applied to every potential use of borrowed capital, without exception and without allowing enthusiasm for a specific opportunity to shortcut the assessment.

The return test is the most fundamental. The projected return on the asset being acquired must exceed the cost of the borrowing by a margin sufficient to justify the risk and illiquidity involved. In real estate, this means the rental income, net of all carrying costs including mortgage payment, property taxes, insurance, maintenance reserves, and vacancy allowance, should produce a positive cash flow or at minimum break even while the asset appreciates. A property that costs money every month to hold is not a wealth-building instrument unless the appreciation is both reliable and substantial enough to compensate — and appreciation, unlike contracted rent, is a projection rather than a certainty. The cash flow calculation must be done honestly, with realistic vacancy rates and maintenance estimates rather than optimistic ones, before any commitment is made.

In business, the return test means the borrowed capital must fund activity that generates revenue exceeding the financing cost within a timeframe that the business's cash position can sustain. Equipment that produces output sold at margins above its financing cost passes. Marketing spend on an unproven channel funded by a business loan does not, because the return is speculative where the cost is contractual.

The resilience test asks what happens when things go worse than expected — not catastrophically, but moderately. Rental property sits vacant for three months rather than two weeks. The business contract falls through. The investment thesis takes longer to materialize than projected. A leveraged position that cannot survive a moderate negative deviation from the base case is not strategic — it is fragile, and fragility in a leveraged position converts moderate setbacks into catastrophic outcomes because the debt obligation continues regardless of the asset's performance. Strategic debt is structured with enough margin between the asset's income and the debt's service cost that temporary underperformance can be absorbed without forcing a distress sale or default.

The expertise test is perhaps the most frequently ignored. Every asset class that can be acquired with leverage — real estate, business equity, securities on margin — has a body of knowledge associated with it that determines the difference between competent and incompetent deployment. Borrowing to invest in an asset class you do not yet understand is not strategic. It is speculation with borrowed money, which concentrates the downside in ways that speculation with only your own capital does not. The appropriate sequence is to acquire genuine understanding of the asset class, ideally through direct involvement at a modest scale before leverage is introduced, and then to apply leverage once the competence to manage the asset and its risks is demonstrably present.

The sleep test gives these principles a human dimension that the mathematics alone cannot capture. If the debt you are considering — the specific amount, at the specific rate, for the specific asset, in the specific circumstances of your current financial life — would cause you to lie awake running calculations and worrying about scenarios, it is wrong for your current stage. Not necessarily wrong forever, not wrong in principle, but wrong now. The sleep test is not about courage or risk tolerance as abstract personality traits. It is about the signal your nervous system sends when the leverage you are considering exceeds what your current financial position, knowledge, and risk capacity can genuinely absorb. Investors who ignore this signal in pursuit of opportunities that seem too good to delay frequently discover that the stress of a leveraged position that exceeds their actual capacity impairs the judgment required to manage it well, creating a self-fulfilling deterioration.

Debt as a spectrum, understood this way, runs from the most destructive consumer instruments at one end — payday loans, revolving credit card balances on consumables, financing on depreciating assets — through the neutral middle ground of necessary borrowing managed carefully, to the genuinely strategic deployment of leverage on productive assets with positive returns, honest risk assessment, and appropriate expertise. Knowing precisely where you currently stand on that spectrum is not a judgment. It is a navigation tool. It tells you whether the next move is elimination, consolidation, or deployment, and it tells you with enough specificity to act on immediately rather than in some better-prepared future that never quite arrives.

The scalpel, in the hands of someone who has learned to use it, does exactly what it was designed to do. So does this.

Chapter 8 — The Law of Invisible Income

8.1 — Money That Moves While You Sleep

There is a particular kind of wealth that does not announce itself. It does not arrive in a visible paycheck, does not require its owner to be present at a specific location at a specific time, and does not stop when the owner stops working. It flows through bank accounts in amounts that vary month to month, generated by assets and arrangements that were built or acquired at some earlier point and now operate with minimal ongoing attention. The person receiving it might be asleep, traveling, ill, or simply living their life by whatever definition they prefer, and the income arrives regardless. To their neighbors, colleagues, and even close friends, the source of this financial stability is often entirely invisible — because it bears no resemblance to the employment model that most people understand as the only legitimate mechanism for earning money.

This invisibility is not accidental, and it is not a consequence of secrecy or deception. It is a natural result of the fact that passive and semi-passive income streams simply do not look like work in any way that the conventional understanding of earning recognizes. There is no commute, no manager, no timesheet, no performance review. There is an asset — intellectual, physical, financial, or digital — that delivers value to other people and receives compensation for doing so, repeatedly, without requiring its owner to personally execute the delivery each time. The income is invisible because the labor that generated it happened in the past, and the ongoing income is the return on that past labor rather than payment for present effort.

The distinction between this model and the time-for-wages model explored in Chapter Four is not merely philosophical. It is the difference between a financial life that is bounded by the hours you can physically work and a financial life that is bounded by the assets you have built — and assets, unlike hours, can accumulate without limit and generate returns simultaneously rather than sequentially. A person with five income streams generating modest amounts each is not just better positioned than a person with one large paycheck. They are structurally different, in a way that becomes most apparent during the moments when financial lives are tested: illness, redundancy, economic disruption, the simple desire to do less.

Understanding why most people never build invisible income requires returning to the educational gap established in the book's opening chapters. The time-for-wages model was what schools prepared students for, what parents modeled in most households, and what the employment economy reinforced through its entire organizational structure. The concept of building assets that generate returns independently was simply absent from the curriculum — not because it was considered and rejected, but because it existed in a different world from the one that mass education was designed to populate. The result is that the majority of working adults have never seriously considered whether passive income was available to them, because the question itself never formed. You cannot pursue an option whose existence was never introduced.

The income ladder is the framework that makes the territory navigable, because passive and semi-passive income is not a single category but a spectrum of arrangements that differ significantly in the amount of ongoing involvement they require, the capital or effort needed to establish them, and the reliability and scalability of the income they produce. Understanding where different streams sit on this ladder allows a person to identify which ones are accessible at their current stage and which ones represent the next step after the initial ones are established.

At the bottom of the ladder sits active income — the time-for-wages model in its purest form. An hour of work produces a unit of pay. No work produces nothing. This is the starting point for most people and the source of the capital and expertise that eventually funds the rungs above it. There is no shame in active income and no suggestion here that it should be abandoned before the alternatives are established. It is simply the first rung, not the destination.

The first step above pure active income is what might be called leveraged active income — arrangements in which the work performed once generates returns that extend beyond the single instance of its performance. A consultant who develops a proprietary methodology and charges for access to it is earning more per hour than a consultant selling undifferentiated advice. A tradesperson who trains and manages a small team is generating income from the team's hours in addition to their own. A freelancer who productizes a service — turning a customized, time-intensive offering into a standardized, efficiently deliverable package — has increased the number of clients they can serve without proportionally increasing the time required. These arrangements still require active participation but begin to decouple income from a strict one-to-one relationship with hours.

The next rung is semi-passive income, where ongoing involvement is required but is substantially less than the income generated might suggest. Rental property is the canonical example. A landlord with a well-selected property, a reliable tenant, and a competent property manager may spend a few hours per month on oversight and decision-making while the property generates monthly rental income, builds equity through mortgage amortization, and appreciates in value. The work required to establish the position — the research, the financing, the acquisition, the initial tenant placement — was substantial. The ongoing maintenance of the income stream, once the system is functioning, is modest. A content creator whose body of work continues to attract new audiences and generate advertising revenue or subscription income years after the content was produced occupies a similar position. The income is not fully passive — new content or audience engagement is periodically required to maintain relevance — but the ratio of ongoing effort to ongoing income is substantially better than any active employment arrangement.

Dividend income from an equity portfolio sits higher on the ladder toward genuinely passive. Companies that pay regular dividends distribute a portion of their earnings to shareholders without requiring those shareholders to perform any function beyond holding the shares. A portfolio of dividend-paying equities or a dividend-focused index fund generates quarterly or monthly income entirely automatically, requiring nothing of the investor except the initial decision to own the assets. The limitation is the capital required to generate meaningful income at typical dividend yields — a portfolio yielding three percent annually requires substantial assets to produce an income worth noting — which is why dividend income tends to become significant later in the wealth-building journey, when the compounding engine of Chapter Six has had sufficient time to accumulate a base large enough to generate meaningful distributions.

Royalty income — from intellectual property including written works, music, patents, software, photography, and an expanding range of digital assets — represents one of the most scalable forms of invisible income available, and one of the most accessible to people who do not begin with significant capital. The mechanism is straightforward: you create something once, license others to use it, and receive payment each time that use occurs. A textbook author receives royalties on every copy sold, potentially for decades after the writing is complete. A photographer whose images are licensed through stock agencies receives a small payment each time an image is downloaded, across a portfolio that can accumulate thousands of images over years of intermittent addition. A software developer whose tool is sold on a marketplace receives revenue from every purchase without involvement in the individual transaction. The common thread is creation followed by licensing — the conversion of expertise and effort into an asset that the market will pay to access repeatedly.

Digital assets represent the newest and most rapidly evolving category on the income ladder, and they deserve mention not because they are universally accessible or universally appropriate but because they have lowered certain barriers to entry that previously made passive income creation the exclusive domain of people with significant capital or established credentials. An online course that teaches a skill the creator has developed through genuine experience can generate enrollment revenue indefinitely once built. A newsletter that develops a loyal readership can be monetized through subscriptions, sponsorships, or affiliated recommendations long after its initial content calendar has been established. A software tool built to solve a specific problem the creator personally experienced can be sold to others experiencing the same problem without the creator's ongoing involvement in each transaction.

The income ladder is not a prescription for simultaneous construction of all rungs. It is a map that shows where you are, where the next step is located, and what it requires to climb to it. Most people who successfully build invisible income begin by establishing one stream — typically the one most accessible given their existing skills, time, and capital — and use the income and knowledge from that first stream to fund and inform the construction of the next. The ladder is climbed one rung at a time, and the view from each successive rung reveals opportunities that were invisible from below.

What the wealthiest people understood, and what the time-for-wages model systematically obscures, is that income does not require presence. It requires assets. And assets, unlike hours, can be built.

8.2 — Three Paths to Your First Invisible Income Stream

The most common reason people never begin building passive income is not laziness and not lack of opportunity. It is the paralysis that comes from looking at the full landscape of possibilities without a clear sense of which entry point corresponds to their actual situation. The person with ten thousand dollars in savings and no particular digital skills is not in the same starting position as the person with deep expertise in a niche field and no capital, and neither is in the same position as the person with a stable income, reasonable credit, and the appetite for a longer-horizon commitment. Treating passive income as a single undifferentiated goal produces a generic roadmap that fits nobody's actual circumstances well enough to follow. The three paths that follow are built around starting conditions rather than ideal scenarios, which means at least one of them describes where you actually are rather than where you wish you were.

The asset path is the most mathematically straightforward and the least dependent on any particular skill or creative capacity. Its core mechanism is capital allocation — directing money into assets that generate returns without requiring ongoing labor — and it is the path most naturally connected to the retention and compounding systems established in earlier chapters. The minimum requirement is capital, which means it is not the first path for someone whose immediate priority is still building the survival buffer and initial growth account. But for anyone who has established those foundations and is beginning to accumulate investable assets, the asset path is the most reliable entry into invisible income because its returns are the most predictable and its execution the least dependent on factors outside the investor's control.

The asset path begins with dividend-generating index funds or individual dividend stocks inside a tax-advantaged account, which produces the first genuinely passive income most people will ever receive — distributions deposited automatically into the account without any action required. The income at this stage is modest, often frustratingly so, but the habit and the structure are what matter in the early years. As the asset base grows, the monthly or quarterly distributions grow proportionally, and at some threshold — different for everyone depending on living costs and income needs — the distributions begin to constitute a meaningful supplement to active income rather than merely a number on a statement.

Real estate enters the asset path when sufficient capital exists for a down payment and the expertise requirements discussed in the previous chapter have been met through genuine research and ideally mentorship from someone with direct experience. The timeline from initial capital accumulation to a functioning rental property generating net positive cash flow is typically two to four years for someone starting from a position of modest savings, accounting for the time required to build the down payment, research markets, identify suitable properties, secure financing, and manage the initial setup. It is not a rapid path, but it is a durable one, and each property acquired, when selected correctly, both generates ongoing income and builds equity that funds the next acquisition.

The creation path requires the least capital of the three and the most honest assessment of what you actually know and can teach, build, or document in a form that others will pay to access. Its minimum requirement is genuine expertise — not world-class mastery, but knowledge or skill that demonstrably exceeds what your target audience currently possesses and that they have a recognized need or desire to acquire. The misunderstanding that stops most people from pursuing this path is the belief that their knowledge must be exceptional or unique to be commercially viable. It does not need to be exceptional. It needs to be useful to a specific group of people who lack it and are willing to pay for access.

A nurse who has spent fifteen years navigating a specific specialty and understands its practical realities in ways that textbooks don't capture has creation path material. A parent who has developed an effective system for managing a particular childhood challenge that other parents consistently struggle with has creation path material. A small business owner who built a functional marketing system for a local service business, through trial and error over several years, has creation path material. The commercial question is not whether the knowledge is impressive in absolute terms. It is whether a defined group of people would pay a reasonable amount to access it in organized form rather than spending the time and money to acquire it through experience themselves.

The primary vehicles on the creation path are digital courses, ebooks, templates, software tools, stock creative assets, and licensing arrangements — each of which shares the fundamental structure of creation followed by repeated sale or licensing without proportional ongoing effort. The timeline from beginning to first meaningful revenue on this path is typically six to eighteen months, which is longer than most people expect and shorter than most people fear. The first three months are consumed by identifying the specific problem to solve and the specific audience experiencing it, validating that the audience exists and will pay before building anything substantial, and creating an initial version of the asset. The following three to six months involve getting the asset into the hands of paying customers, gathering feedback, and iterating toward a version that delivers reliable results. The period after that is about distribution — expanding the channels through which potential customers discover the asset — which is where the income begins to scale beyond what direct, one-at-a-time marketing can produce.

The ownership path covers small business acquisition and real estate beyond single rental properties, and it requires the most capital, the most management involvement, and the longest timeline of the three. It is also the path with the highest income ceiling, because the leverage available through business ownership and larger property portfolios is substantially greater than what individual asset accumulation or digital product creation typically produces. A small business acquired at a reasonable multiple of its earnings, with competent management installed or developed, generates owner income that is structurally similar to passive income — the owner receives distributions from the business's earnings without performing the daily operational work. This is the model that creates many of the most significant personal fortunes that appear, from the outside, to have arrived without obvious corresponding effort.

The minimum requirements for the ownership path are significant: typically a combination of capital for acquisition or down payment, creditworthiness for business or real estate financing, sufficient management experience to evaluate and oversee an operation without running it personally, and the patience for a timeline that runs three to seven years from initial position to a genuinely self-managing income stream. It is not an appropriate first path for most people reading this book, but understanding it as a destination — the rung several steps above the current one — provides the longer-horizon context that makes the earlier steps feel purposeful rather than merely preparatory.

Chapter 9 — The Law of Protective Barriers

9.1 — The Bucket With Holes

There is a particular financial tragedy that receives almost no attention in conventional wealth-building literature, possibly because it is less inspiring than the accumulation story and more uncomfortable to examine. It is the tragedy of the person who built something — who spent years doing the right things, retaining income, investing consistently, developing income streams, watching the compounding curve begin to bend upward — and then lost a substantial portion of it, or all of it, to something that was entirely preventable. Not a market crash, which is an accepted risk of participation. Not a business failure, which is an accepted risk of entrepreneurship. Something structural — a medical emergency that consumed savings built over a decade, a lawsuit that reached personal assets because the right legal structure was not in place, an estate that passed to the wrong people or was consumed by taxes and legal fees because no document existed to direct it otherwise, a tax bill that arrived because legal optimization strategies the accountant assumed the client knew about were never discussed.

These are not rare outcomes. They are common enough that any honest financial advisor will have multiple examples from their own client history, and they share a characteristic that makes them particularly painful: they were avoidable. The wealth existed. The threat existed. The barrier that would have stood between them was not built, and so when the threat arrived — as it always eventually does in one form or another — it passed directly through to the asset.

Building wealth without protecting it is, in the most literal functional sense, filling a bucket with holes. The filling can be diligent, skilled, and sustained over many years, and the bucket can still be empty at the end if the holes are large enough and the water pressure of circumstance is eventually applied to them. The law of protective barriers is the discipline of finding and closing those holes before circumstance finds them for you.

There are four essential barriers, and they are presented here in the order of their accessibility and urgency rather than their theoretical importance, because a framework that begins with the most complex and least immediately achievable element tends to produce inaction at every level. Each barrier is buildable by an ordinary person with ordinary income at ordinary stages of wealth accumulation. None of them require the wealth to already be substantial to justify their construction. The barrier is most valuable when built before it is needed, which by definition means building it before the asset base that seems to warrant it has arrived.

The first barrier is the emergency fund, which was introduced in Chapter Five as the survival account — the first tier of the retention system. It reappears here not as repetition but as completion, because the survival account was discussed in the context of retention mechanics and it deserves a second examination in the context of protection. The function of a properly sized emergency fund is not merely to prevent the inconvenience of unexpected expenses. It is to prevent the forced liquidation of long-term assets at precisely the wrong moment — which is also, because financial emergencies and market downturns have an unfortunate tendency to coincide, likely to be the worst possible moment to sell.

The correct sizing of an emergency fund is more context-dependent than the standard three-to-six-month prescription suggests. Three months is appropriate for a household with two stable incomes, low fixed costs, and an employment market where comparable work can be found relatively quickly if one income is lost. Six months is more appropriate for a single-income household, a self-employed individual whose income is variable, or anyone in a specialized field where replacement income might take longer to establish. Beyond six months becomes appropriate for business owners whose personal finances are intertwined with the business's cash position, for anyone carrying significant fixed obligations that would immediately become unmanageable without income, and for anyone whose industry is experiencing structural disruption that makes income instability a realistic near-term risk. The emergency fund is not an investment. Optimizing its yield is a secondary consideration. Its primary requirement is that it exists in full, in a liquid form that is accessible within forty-eight hours, and that it is sized to the actual structure of your financial life rather than a generic prescription written for someone else's.

The second barrier is insurance, and this is where the most significant miseducation occurs — not through absence of information, but through the deliberate overcomplication of a topic that benefits enormously from simplicity. The insurance industry is structured to sell products, and the products it most profitably sells are not always the ones that most efficiently protect the people buying them. The result is a market in which the genuinely necessary forms of insurance are sometimes underowned while the expensive and unnecessary ones are enthusiastically pushed, and the average person, equipped with no framework for distinguishing between them, makes decisions based on whatever the last salesperson explained most compellingly.

The framework for evaluating insurance is straightforward and cuts through virtually all of the industry's complexity: insure against financial losses that you could not absorb without serious and lasting damage to your financial position. Do not insure against losses that you could absorb from savings or income without lasting damage, because doing so transfers your money to an insurer at a price that is guaranteed to exceed the expected value of the claims you will make — that differential is literally the insurer's profit margin.

Applied to specific products, this framework produces clear direction. Health insurance is non-negotiable in any system where a serious medical event produces bills that could consume years of savings — which describes most countries outside those with comprehensive universal coverage, and even within universal systems, supplemental coverage for income replacement during extended illness is worth examining. Disability insurance is the most underowned form of protection among working adults, and its absence represents the largest single gap in most people's protective barrier. The statistical probability of experiencing a disability lasting more than ninety days at some point during a working career is considerably higher than most people estimate, and the financial consequence of that disability without income replacement insurance — the cessation of all earned income while fixed expenses continue — is severe enough to unwind years of wealth accumulation in a matter of months.

Life insurance serves a specific and limited purpose: replacing income that dependents rely on if the earner dies prematurely. Term life insurance — a policy that pays a death benefit during a defined period at a fixed premium — serves this purpose efficiently and inexpensively. Permanent life insurance products, including whole life and universal life variants, combine an insurance function with an investment function in ways that typically serve neither as well as keeping them separate, and they carry costs that make them significantly more expensive than equivalent term coverage for most buyers in most circumstances. The appropriate amount of term coverage is typically a multiple of annual income sufficient to replace the earner's financial contribution to the household during the period when dependents remain reliant on it. When the children are independent and the mortgage is retired and the investment portfolio has grown to a point where it can itself support the surviving partner, the need for life insurance diminishes substantially and may disappear entirely.

Property and liability insurance protect against the specific risk of asset loss — home, vehicle, and the liability exposure that comes with owning property and operating in the world in ways that could result in legal claims. Umbrella liability coverage, which extends protection beyond the limits of underlying home and auto policies, is one of the most cost-effective protective barriers available and one of the least discussed. For modest annual premiums, it provides several million dollars of additional liability coverage that stands between a single adverse legal judgment and the personal assets built over years of disciplined accumulation.

The third barrier is estate planning, and its neglect among people who do not yet consider themselves wealthy is one of the most consequential financial errors that does not feel like one in the moment. The perception that estate planning is for people with large estates is understandable but wrong, because the problems that estate planning solves are not primarily about the size of the estate. They are about who controls your assets if you become incapacitated, who receives them when you die, who makes medical decisions on your behalf if you cannot make them yourself, and who cares for your children if both parents die while the children are still minors.

A will is the foundational document — the instruction that directs the distribution of your assets according to your wishes rather than the default rules of the jurisdiction you inhabit, which distribute assets according to a formula that may bear no relationship to your actual intentions. A power of attorney designates someone to manage your financial affairs if you become unable to do so. A healthcare directive specifies your medical wishes and designates someone to make healthcare decisions when you cannot. For parents of minor children, a will is also the document that names a guardian — the person who will raise your children if you do not — and its absence means that decision is made by a court applying statutory criteria rather than by you.

These documents are not expensive to create, are not complicated to understand in their basic form, and do not require a large estate to justify. They require only the recognition that the decisions they address are inevitable — you will die, you may become incapacitated, your assets will transfer to someone — and that the question is not whether those events will be managed but whether they will be managed according to your wishes or according to default rules written for no one in particular.

The fourth barrier is tax optimization — and the distinction between optimization and evasion deserves immediate and unambiguous establishment. Evasion is illegal concealment of income or assets from tax authorities. Optimization is the entirely legal use of available structures, allowances, deductions, and timing strategies to minimize the tax burden on income and wealth within the rules the system provides. Every jurisdiction's tax code contains provisions that the legislature deliberately created to encourage certain behaviors — retirement saving, charitable giving, business investment, homeownership in many systems — and using those provisions as intended is not aggressive or ethically questionable. It is financial literacy applied to one of the largest costs most people will pay across a lifetime.

The most powerful tax optimization available to most people is also the most straightforward: maximizing contributions to tax-advantaged accounts before directing money to taxable ones. The difference in after-tax, after-compounding returns between money held inside a tax-advantaged account and identical money held in a taxable account, over a thirty-year investment period, is substantial enough that failing to use available allowances fully is the functional equivalent of voluntarily paying a significant additional tax. Beyond account optimization, understanding the tax treatment of different income types — the difference between ordinary income rates and capital gains rates, the deductibility of business expenses for self-employed individuals, the tax implications of different investment structures — provides additional optimization that accumulates meaningfully over years without requiring any arrangement more complex than basic financial organization.

The four barriers, built in sequence and maintained with reasonable attention, do not guarantee that nothing will ever go wrong. They guarantee that if something goes wrong, it will encounter resistance before it reaches the assets built through years of disciplined accumulation. That resistance — the emergency fund absorbing the blow, the insurance covering the loss, the legal structure protecting the asset, the tax efficiency compounding the retained return — is the difference between a setback and a catastrophe.

The bucket, properly sealed, holds what you put into it.

9.2 — The Wealth Destroyers Nobody Warns You About

Building the four protective barriers of the previous section addresses the structural vulnerabilities in a financial life — the holes that can be identified, measured, and closed through deliberate action. But there is a second category of wealth destruction that operates differently, arriving not through identifiable gaps in legal or financial structure but through behavioral patterns and relational dynamics that are harder to see clearly because they feel, in the moment of their operation, like normal life. These destroyers do not announce themselves. They arrive wearing the clothes of celebration, loyalty, excitement, or opportunity, and they extract wealth through mechanisms that bypass the rational financial mind entirely.

Lifestyle inflation is the most statistically significant of the four, measured by the sheer number of people it affects and the cumulative magnitude of its extraction over a career. Every income increase creates a new margin — a gap between previous spending and new earning — and that margin is, at the moment of its creation, genuinely unallocated. The question of where it goes is decided in the weeks and months following the raise, the promotion, the new contract, and it is decided largely through a combination of social comparison, accumulated deprivation, and the entirely human desire to let improved circumstances be felt in daily life.

The inflation happens incrementally and therefore invisibly. The apartment upgrade seems reasonable given the new income. The car replacement is justifiable — the old one was aging. The dining habits shift upward, the wardrobe improves, the holidays become more elaborate, the subscriptions accumulate. Each individual adjustment is defensible. Their aggregate effect is the permanent consumption of the new margin, leaving the retention rate unchanged despite the income increase, and repeating this pattern across multiple income increases over a career produces the outcome examined in the compounding chapter: a person earning three times their starting salary whose financial position has not improved proportionally because spending expanded to meet each income increase before retention could claim it.

The prevention protocol is a commitment made before the income increase arrives rather than after it lands. Specifically:

when income increases by any amount, a minimum of fifty percent of the net increase is automatically redirected to the growth account before the new income level is experienced as available spending. The lifestyle improvement then comes from the remaining fifty percent, which is still a genuine improvement and one that can be enjoyed without the financial cost of absorbing the entire increase. This commitment is not made in the moment of receiving good news, when the temptation to celebrate fully is at its most powerful. It is made during a calm planning session and written down with sufficient specificity — the percentage, the account, the date the automatic transfer will be adjusted — that execution requires no additional decision-making when the moment arrives.

Toxic financial relationships represent a category of wealth destruction that personal finance literature has historically handled with such delicacy that it fails to convey the actual magnitude of the risk. The relationships in question are not limited to romantic partnerships, though those carry the highest financial stakes given the legal entanglement of shared finances and the emotional complexity of money conversations with intimate partners. They include family members whose financial dysfunction becomes the default beneficiary of your financial progress, friendships whose social rituals are organized around spending levels you cannot sustain without damaging your own position, and business or professional relationships in which one party's financial benefit is systematically extracted from the other's.

The specific pattern to identify is persistent one-directionality: financial resources consistently flowing from you toward another person or relationship without meaningful reciprocation, and the expectation of that flow being reinforced by guilt, obligation, or the implicit threat of relational consequences if it stops. A parent who treats an adult child's financial stability as a resource to be drawn upon for their own needs, a partner who spends freely while leaving savings to the other party, a social group whose spending norms require financial performance that exceeds your actual position — each of these relationships, maintained without boundaries, functions as a direct drain on the retention system built in Chapter Five.

The prevention protocol requires two things that are genuinely difficult in practice and worth doing anyway. The first is clarity about what you can actually afford to give, lend, or spend in any relationship — not what would be expected, not what would prevent conflict, but what your actual financial position supports without damaging your trajectory. The second is the communication of that boundary with the same matter-of-fact directness you would apply to any other factual constraint. The most financially protective response to a request that exceeds your boundary is not an elaborate justification or an apologetic refusal. It is a simple statement of what you can and cannot do, delivered without excessive explanation, followed by consistency in maintaining it regardless of the pressure applied.

Emotional investing is the third destroyer, and it operates through the most sophisticated manipulation available to any wealth-destroying force — your own psychology, applied against your own interests with the assistance of media, markets, and the opinions of people who are themselves in the grip of the same emotional state. The two primary emotional conditions that destroy investment returns are fear during market downturns and euphoria during market expansions, and they produce opposite behaviors that share the same mathematical consequence: selling when prices are low and buying when prices are high.

During a significant market decline, the emotional experience of watching an investment portfolio lose value produces a pain response that behavioral economists have documented extensively. Losses feel roughly twice as painful as equivalent gains feel pleasurable — a finding so consistent across populations and contexts that it functions almost as a psychological constant. This asymmetry means that during a sharp decline, the emotional pressure to sell — to stop the pain, to preserve what remains — is disproportionately powerful relative to the rational analysis that would recommend holding or adding to positions at lower prices. The investors who sell during downturns are not irrational people failing to apply knowledge they possess. They are people whose emotional response to loss is overriding their intellectual understanding of market cycles, and the override happens fast enough that the rational mind often constructs a justification for the emotional decision after the fact.

During market expansions and bubbles, the equivalent emotional state is euphoria combined with social contagion — the experience of watching prices rise, hearing accounts of others' gains, and feeling that not participating more aggressively is itself a form of loss. This produces the mirror behavior: purchasing assets at elevated prices, often with leverage, in a market where the risk-reward relationship has deteriorated significantly from the conditions that would have made the investment attractive.

The prevention protocol for emotional investing is structural rather than psychological, because attempting to override emotional responses through willpower in the moment they are operating is a losing strategy against a force that evolution has spent millions of years reinforcing. The structure consists of three elements: a written investment policy that specifies what you own, why you own it, and under what predetermined conditions you would change it; automatic investment contributions that continue regardless of market conditions without requiring a decision in each period; and a self-imposed rule against checking portfolio values more frequently than quarterly, which eliminates most of the emotional stimuli that trigger reactive decisions. The policy is the rational mind speaking to the emotional mind in advance, before the emotional conditions that impair judgment have arrived.

Fraud and scam vulnerability is the fourth destroyer, and its inclusion here is not a comment on the intelligence or sophistication of the people who fall victim to it. Fraud is a professional industry staffed by people who study human psychology with the specific aim of exploiting it, and its techniques have become sufficiently refined that they regularly defeat highly educated and financially experienced individuals. The profiles of fraud victims documented by consumer protection agencies consistently show that education and income provide considerably less protection than people expect.

The specific patterns most dangerous to wealth-builders are investment fraud — schemes that promise returns substantially above what legitimate markets produce and use the early investors' apparent gains to recruit further participants before collapsing — and impersonation fraud, in which criminals present themselves as financial institutions, government agencies, or trusted professional relationships to extract account access or direct fund transfers. The emotional lever most commonly applied in both categories is urgency: the opportunity will disappear, the account will be closed, the legal consequence will occur if you do not act immediately. Urgency is the mechanism by which the fraud removes the pause that would allow rational evaluation to function.

The prevention protocol is a single rule applied without exception: any financial decision involving a significant sum requires a waiting period of at least twenty-four hours and verification of all parties through independently sourced contact information — not the number or link provided in the communication that prompted the decision, but the number you find independently through official channels. Legitimate opportunities tolerate waiting. Legitimate institutions welcome verification. Any pressure to act before you have completed both is itself the most reliable indicator that the situation is not what it is presented to be.

Chapter 10 — The Law of Infinite Players

10.1 — The Game Within the Game

Most people relate to money through a series of finite goals. Pay off the car. Save enough for the holiday. Get to a point where the credit card is clear. Reach a balance that feels like safety. Buy the house. Retire at a specific age with a specific number. Each of these goals has a defined endpoint, a condition of completion, a moment at which the game is won and can be set down. This is a natural and understandable way to relate to a resource that presents itself primarily as a solution to immediate and near-term problems, and there is nothing wrong with finite goals as organizational tools for specific financial decisions. The problem is when the finite goal structure becomes the entire framework through which a person relates to their financial life — when winning the current game is treated as the purpose of the enterprise rather than one move within a much longer one.

The philosopher James Carse drew a distinction, in a short and quietly influential book published in 1986, between finite games and infinite games that illuminates this problem with particular clarity when applied to wealth. Finite games are played to win: they have defined rules, agreed boundaries, a clear conclusion, and a winner who achieves the objective before the game ends. Infinite games are played to continue: their purpose is not to reach a conclusion but to sustain the play itself, to keep as many participants as possible in the game for as long as possible, evolving the rules as necessary to prevent the game from ending. Applied to wealth, the distinction describes two fundamentally different orientations toward money and time — orientations that produce dramatically different outcomes over the long periods during which financial lives actually unfold.

The finite player optimizes for the current goal. When the goal is paying off debt, every decision is evaluated through the lens of debt reduction. When the goal is saving for a house, every decision is evaluated through the lens of the down payment. This is not wrong in the short term — focus on a specific objective is genuinely useful for achieving it. The limitation appears at the conclusion of each goal, because the finite player who achieves their objective has no larger game into which the victory fits. The debt is paid, and without a framework for what the freed cash flow now builds, it dissolves back into spending. The house is purchased, and the equity accumulating within it is not consciously connected to a longer-horizon wealth architecture that would direct it toward the next asset. The retirement number is reached, and without an infinite framework for managing and deploying that wealth across a potentially multi-decade retirement, it is managed reactively rather than strategically.

The infinite player relates to money differently from the beginning. Each specific financial goal is not the game — it is a position within a game that does not end with any single achievement. Paying off destructive debt is not the destination. It is the move that frees cash flow for the next position. Buying the first property is not the conclusion. It is the entry point into a system of asset accumulation that was always designed to extend beyond the first acquisition. Reaching financial independence is not the finish line. It is the moment at which the rules of the game shift from accumulation to stewardship and legacy — the beginning of a new phase rather than the end of the enterprise.

The historical evidence for this distinction's importance is not subtle. The families and dynasties that have maintained significant wealth across multiple generations — the merchant families of Renaissance Europe, the landed estates that survived centuries of economic disruption, the industrial families whose fortunes persisted through successors who neither built them nor destroyed them — share a characteristic that is visible in retrospect across all of them. They did not think about money in years. They thought about money in decades, and the most durable among them thought in generations — a time horizon so extended that the individual making decisions would not live to see their full expression.

This generational thinking manifests in specific, practical ways that distinguish it sharply from even the most sophisticated short-horizon financial planning. The infinite player invests in assets whose full value will not be realized during their lifetime — trees whose shade they will not sit under, in the agricultural metaphor that recurs across many cultures' wisdom traditions. They make decisions about legal structures, family governance, and wealth management with explicit attention to how those decisions will function when the current decision-maker is no longer present. They educate their children not merely in the vocational skills that will produce income in the next generation but in the financial principles that will preserve and extend wealth across the generation after that. They think about reputation, relationship, and institutional trust as assets that compound across time in the same way that financial capital compounds — slowly at first, then with a momentum that becomes nearly impossible to halt.

The Rothschild banking family, whose trajectory from a Frankfurt ghetto in the late eighteenth century to a multi-generational European financial empire represents one of the most studied examples of sustained wealth creation in history, operated explicitly by an infinite game philosophy that was articulated within the family as a governing principle rather than left as an implicit assumption. The founding patriarch Mayer Amschel Rothschild is reported to have told his sons that concordance among family members was more valuable than any single financial advantage — a statement that prioritizes the continuity of the game over the winning of any individual round within it. Whether the precise words are accurately attributed matters less than the documented fact that the family operated for generations according to a philosophy that was explicitly longer-horizon than any individual member's lifetime.

The Rockefeller family's management of its wealth across four generations provides a more extensively documented example of the same philosophy at work in a different cultural context. The organizational structures created to manage and perpetuate the family's wealth — the family office model, the philanthropic foundations, the explicit financial education of successive generations — were not primarily tax-minimization strategies, though they served that function. They were the architectural expression of an infinite game philosophy: the deliberate construction of systems designed to persist and function beyond any individual player's participation in them. The wealth was not merely accumulated. It was institutionalized — given structures and governance mechanisms that could carry it forward independently of the specific people who happened to be managing it at any given moment.

The objection that these examples are drawn from families of extraordinary initial wealth — that the infinite game is available only to those who have already won sufficiently large finite games — misunderstands the relationship between the philosophy and the outcome. The infinite game orientation is not the result of great wealth. It is, in significant part, a cause of it. The families that built multi-generational wealth were not infinite players because they were already wealthy. They became sustainably wealthy because they were already infinite players — because their orientation toward money and time was already extended beyond the current goal, beyond the current generation, beyond the current game, before the wealth reached a scale that made this perspective seem obviously justified.

This matters practically because it means the infinite game is available to anyone at any financial stage, and its adoption does not require waiting until wealth is established to justify the longer horizon. The person with a modest investment account who has decided that account is the beginning of a family financial legacy — not a retirement nest egg to be consumed in one generation but the foundation of a wealth-building tradition to be extended and passed forward — is already playing a different game than their financial circumstances would suggest. The decisions that flow from that orientation are different from the decisions that flow from a single-generation retirement focus, even when the current financial position is identical. The infinite player makes different choices about what to retain, what to invest, what to teach, what to structure legally, and how to think about the relationship between present consumption and future endowment.

The most expensive financial belief most people carry is not any specific misconception about interest rates or investment vehicles. It is the belief that their financial life is a problem to be solved — that there is a number, a condition, a moment of completion toward which they are working, after which the financial question can be set aside. This belief ensures that whatever is built will be built for one lifetime, consumed in one lifetime, and leave nothing behind but the absence of the burden it once represented.

The alternative is not a sacrifice. It is an expansion. An expansion of time horizon, of purpose, of the relationship between current action and future consequence. It is the recognition that the game you are playing does not have to end with you — that wealth, built correctly and oriented correctly, is not a finite resource to be accumulated and spent but an infinite capacity to be developed and extended.

The game within the game is the one that matters most. It is the one that most people never knew they were allowed to play.

10.2 — Becoming an Infinite Player

The shift from finite to infinite thinking is not a single decision so much as a progressive reorientation — a gradual expansion of the time horizon through which financial decisions are evaluated, until the expansion becomes habitual enough to function as a default rather than a deliberate override. It does not happen automatically as wealth accumulates, because wealth without philosophy simply produces larger versions of the same finite games. It happens through deliberate practice of three specific disciplines that, taken together, restructure the relationship between present action and future consequence in a way that eventually becomes self-sustaining.

The first discipline is the twenty-five-year financial vision, and its value is in direct proportion to the discomfort most people feel when first attempting it. Five-year plans are uncomfortable enough — they require projecting across a period long enough that genuine uncertainty exists about circumstances, opportunities, and priorities. Twenty-five years extends that projection into territory that feels almost fictional, which is precisely where its power resides. A twenty-five-year financial vision is not a forecast. It is a statement of direction — the orientation from which every shorter-horizon decision derives its meaning and toward which every incremental action contributes its small momentum.

The exercise begins not with numbers but with a description of what financial freedom, fully realized, actually looks like in a life that is yours specifically. Not a generic wealthy life borrowed from aspirational media — your life, with your values, your relationships, your preferred texture of daily existence, your sense of what constitutes genuine contribution and meaning. This description exists at a level of detail that makes it imaginable rather than merely conceptual: where you are, what you are doing with your time, what financial structures are generating the income that makes those choices available, who is in your life and in what relationship to your wealth, and what you are building that will persist beyond the period you personally inhabit. The numbers come after the description, derived from it rather than imposed upon it, because numbers without the life they are meant to fund are targets without destinations.

From the twenty-five-year vision, the intermediate milestones become visible and meaningful in a way they cannot be when they exist only as isolated goals. The ten-year position required to be on track for the twenty-five-year vision, the five-year position required to reach the ten-year milestone, the one-year position required to be building toward the five-year one — each intermediate point is not a separate game but a confirmed position within the single extended game. This nested structure prevents the disorientation that accompanies the achievement of any single goal, because completion is never the end of the game. It is evidence of movement within it.

The second discipline is system design that outlasts motivation, which is the infinite player's solution to the problem that finite players solve with willpower. Motivation is a finite resource. It arrives strongly at the beginning of a new commitment, diminishes through the middle period when early enthusiasm has faded and results have not yet arrived, and requires renewal that cannot always be reliably produced on demand. A financial system that depends on sustained motivation to function will fail at the statistical rate at which motivation fails, which is high enough to be the primary cause of most abandoned financial plans.

The infinite player designs systems that run without their active participation in each cycle — automatic contributions, automatic rebalancing, automatic protection reviews on a calendar schedule, automatic escalation of retention rates tied to income review dates. These systems do not require motivation to operate. They require only the initial motivation to design and implement them, and the periodic motivation to review and adjust them as circumstances change. Between those review points, they run independently, accumulating the patient, consistent progress that finite motivation-dependent approaches attempt and fail to sustain.

The third discipline — and the one that most distinctively characterizes infinite game thinking at its most developed — is the personal wealth constitution: a written document that articulates the financial principles by which you have decided to live, expressed with sufficient specificity and conviction that it functions as a governing framework for financial decisions made under conditions of emotional pressure, social influence, or temporary confusion about priorities.

The concept of a wealth constitution draws on the observation that the moments when financial principles are most needed are precisely the moments when they are most difficult to access — when markets are falling and the instinct to sell is overwhelming, when a compelling opportunity arrives with urgency attached, when a relationship creates pressure to violate a financial boundary, when a windfall creates sudden access to spending that the retention system was designed to prevent. In these moments, having previously committed your principles to writing and articulated the reasoning behind them creates a source of guidance that is more stable than real-time emotional reasoning.

A wealth constitution is structured around a small number of foundational principles — typically between five and ten — each stated with enough specificity to generate clear guidance in concrete situations, and each accompanied by a brief explanation of the reasoning behind it that will be meaningful to the person reading it during a difficult moment. The principles should be genuinely yours — derived from your values, your history, your specific vulnerabilities and strengths — rather than borrowed wholesale from someone else's philosophy. A principle that resonates deeply because it reflects genuine conviction will hold under pressure in a way that a principle adopted because an authority figure recommended it will not.

A template for the structure of each principle within the constitution consists of three components: the principle stated clearly and specifically, the situation in which it is most likely to be tested, and the reason it was established in language that will reconnect the reader to the original conviction. As examples of the kind of specificity that makes a principle operational rather than decorative: "I do not make any financial commitment exceeding a defined threshold without a minimum of seventy-two hours between first exposure and decision, regardless of how the opportunity is framed or who is presenting it" — tested when an investment opportunity arrives with urgency or social pressure, established because the most costly financial decisions in my history were made quickly under external pressure. Or: "I increase my growth account contribution percentage within thirty days of any income increase, before any lifestyle adjustment is made" — tested at every raise or windfall, established because I have watched the alternative produce no improvement in financial position despite significant income growth.

The wealth constitution is a living document — reviewed annually, updated when life circumstances or values shift significantly, and refined as experience generates new conviction about what matters and what doesn't. Its value is not in its permanence but in its existence: the fact that it was written at all, during a moment of calm and clear thinking, means that the calm clear thinking is accessible during the moments when it is most needed.

Conclusion: Your Wealth Begins Now

You began this book being told that most people retire broke not because they lack talent or discipline, but because they were never taught the rules. Everything that followed was the delivery of that promise — not theory constructed for its own intellectual interest, but recovered principle, verified across thousands of years of human financial experience, translated into the language and context of a life being lived right now.

Seven laws. Not seven tips, not seven habits, not seven things wealthy people do before breakfast. Seven foundational principles that governed wealth creation before modern financial products existed, that continued governing it while those products were designed to obscure them, and that govern it still — indifferent to inflation rates, market cycles, technological disruption, and every other variable that financial media presents as the primary determinant of your financial future.

The Law of Financial Identity established that you will never sustainably outperform the wealth thermostat set by your subconscious self-image. Before any tactic can hold, the identity from which it is executed must be capable of sustaining it. The work of resetting that thermostat — through evidence-based affirmation, deliberate environment design, and the disciplined practice of future-self visualization — is not preparation for the real work. It is the real work, and everything built on top of it is only as stable as the identity beneath it.

The Law of Value Creation dismantled the time-for-wages model and replaced it with the income equation that the market actually uses: value delivered equals problem solved multiplied by number of people served multiplied by difficulty of replacement. Earning more is a learnable skill, not a fortunate accident. Skill stacking, problem targeting, and asset creation are the three mechanisms through which any person at any income level can move along that equation in their favor.

The Law of Retention established that wealth is built not by what you earn but by what you keep, and that keeping it requires a structural decision made before spending begins rather than after. The three-tier system — survival account, growth account, freedom account — funded automatically in that sequence, transforms the ancient Babylonian principle of paying yourself first from philosophical advice into operational reality.

The Law of Compounding Forces extended the standard compound interest lesson into its full territory: skills, relationships, and reputation compound by the same mathematics as invested capital, and the flat early portion of the curve — the phase that causes most people to quit — is not evidence of failure. It is the construction phase of everything that follows. The enemies of compounding — inflation, fees, taxes, and lifestyle creep — each have specific countermeasures, and without those shields the engine generates far less than its gross returns suggest.

The Law of Strategic Debt replaced the binary of debt-as-evil and debt-as-normal with the only distinction that produces intelligent decisions: destructive debt finances consumption and drains wealth through compound interest paid in the wrong direction, while strategic debt acquires productive assets whose returns exceed the cost of the borrowing. The cascade method eliminates the first. The return test, the resilience test, the expertise test, and the sleep test govern the second.

The Law of Invisible Income introduced the income ladder from active to fully passive and described the three paths — the asset path, the creation path, and the ownership path — through which any person, at any starting point, can begin building income that does not require their presence for every instance of its delivery. The front-end work is real. The timeline is honest. The structural outcome — income that continues when you cannot or choose not to work — is the bridge between financial stability and genuine financial freedom.

The Law of Protective Barriers completed the architecture by addressing the hole in every wealth-building plan that focuses exclusively on accumulation: building without protecting is filling a bucket with holes. Emergency funds sized correctly to actual circumstances, insurance matched to genuine risk rather than fear-based selling, estate documents that exist before they are urgently needed, tax optimization that uses every legal provision available — these are not afterthoughts. They are the difference between wealth that holds and wealth that evaporates under the first significant pressure circumstance applies.

And beneath all seven laws, the orienting philosophy of the infinite game: the recognition that wealth is not a problem to be solved but a capacity to be developed, not a destination to be reached but a direction to be maintained, not a finite accumulation to be consumed in one lifetime but a compounding legacy to be extended across generations.

The core thesis of this book has not changed from the first page: these laws were always available. They were buried, not destroyed. You have now excavated them. And the excavation changes nothing unless it is followed by the only thing that converts recovered knowledge into actual wealth.

Action. Yours. Beginning now.

Thirty days is not enough time to build wealth. It is enough time to build the systems that build wealth, and systems, once running, do not require the same intensity of attention that their construction demanded. The following sequence is designed to move from zero to operational across every law in this book, prioritized by the order in which each action enables the ones that follow.

In the first week, the work is identity and inventory. On day one, complete the financial script audit from Chapter Three — write every money belief inherited from your upbringing, identify the ones still active in your behavior, and write the replacement identity statement grounded in evidence you can actually point to. On day two, complete the value audit from Chapter Four — answer the three diagnostic questions about what you do with ease that others find difficult, where people seek your help repeatedly, and what experience-based knowledge you carry that most people around you lack. On day three, calculate your actual monthly essential expenses — not total spending, the irreducible minimum — and multiply by the appropriate number of months for your household structure. This is your survival account target. On day four, list every debt instrument you carry with its balance, rate, minimum payment, and monthly interest cost in dollars. On day five, review your insurance coverage against the framework established in Chapter Nine and note every gap. On days six and seven, write the first draft of your twenty-five-year financial vision — not numbers yet, the description of the life — and identify which of the three invisible income paths corresponds most accurately to your current starting position.

In the second week, the work is structural. Open the accounts that the retention system requires if they do not already exist — a survival account at a separate institution from your primary spending account, a growth account or confirmed tax-advantaged investment account. Set up the automatic transfers that fund them, timed to the day income arrives. If the survival account target has not yet been reached, direct the full retained percentage there until it is. Confirm that your growth account contributions are directed to the lowest-cost index funds available within the account, weighted appropriately to your time horizon. If any insurance gaps were identified in week one, initiate the process of addressing the most critical one — disability coverage first if it is absent, then the others in order of the financial damage their absence would permit.

In the third week, the work is income and debt. Apply the cascade method to your debt list: confirm that minimum payments on all debts are being met, identify the highest-rate debt, and direct every available dollar above those minimums to it. Make the rate-negotiation call to the issuer of your highest-rate credit card. On the income side, take the first concrete action corresponding to your chosen invisible income path — not planning the action, the action itself. Open the investment account if the asset path is yours. Begin the audience research and concept validation if the creation path is yours. Identify the first specific market or target to research if the ownership path is yours. The action at this stage will feel small. It is small. It is also the first plank on the bridge.

In the fourth week, the work is protection and constitution. Draft your personal wealth constitution: identify the five to seven financial principles that reflect your genuine convictions, specify the situation in which each is most likely to be tested, and write the reasoning behind each in language that will be meaningful to you during a high-pressure moment. Review the estate planning checklist from Chapter Nine and initiate the creation of any missing documents. Complete the wealth protection audit and convert every identified gap into a dated action item. On the final day of the thirty, review everything built across the month — the accounts, the automation, the debt cascade, the income path begun, the constitution drafted, the protection gaps addressed — and note the distance traveled from day one.

Imperfect execution of this plan in thirty days produces more actual financial progress than perfect planning across six months of continued preparation. The compounding clock is not waiting for your circumstances to improve. It has been running your entire adult life. The question is only whether the engine is now pointing in a direction that benefits you.

Every generation before yours that stayed financially trapped — and there were many, across every culture and income level and era of economic history — did so not because they were less capable, less disciplined, or less deserving. They did so because these laws never found them. The knowledge that was common literacy among Babylonian merchants, Renaissance guild masters, and self-made industrialists was allowed to disappear from the curriculum of ordinary life, and the people who needed it most were left to navigate a sophisticated financial system with no map, no compass, and no honest account of the territory.

You have the map now. You have the compass. You have read the honest account.

The people who built wealth across history were not a different species. They were not born into clarity that you were denied by the accident of circumstance. They were people who, at some moment that felt ordinary from the inside, encountered the principles that govern wealth and made a decision — not a dramatic, cinematic decision, but a quiet and serious one — to let those principles reorganize their relationship with money from that point forward. Some of them encountered the principles young, and the compounding of time worked in their favor with extraordinary force. Some of them encountered them late, and built more than people around them thought possible in the time remaining. The common thread was not the timing. It was the decision.

Your financial story is not written. Whatever has preceded this moment — whatever debt has accumulated, whatever opportunities have been missed, whatever years have passed without the knowledge you now possess — none of it is the conclusion. It is the context. And context, unlike conclusion, can be followed by something different.

The single most powerful thing you can do today, beyond the first actions of the thirty-day plan, is to give this book to one person who needs it. Not to a person who is already financially sophisticated — to the person in your life who is working hard and getting nowhere, who carries financial shame they have never articulated, who has never been offered a real explanation for why the rules seem to work for some people and not for them. Your sibling. Your closest friend. The colleague who mentioned debt in passing and then changed the subject. The parent who is approaching retirement with insufficient savings and no language for what went wrong.

The laws multiplied are more powerful than the laws held. Wealth shared as knowledge costs nothing and compounds in the hands of every person who receives it and acts on it. The greatest financial gift anyone in your life ever gave you would have been this information, delivered early enough to matter. You can be that person for someone else, and you can be it today.

The game is infinite. The laws are recovered. The clock has been running, and it continues to run — in your favor now, rather than against you, because the difference between those two directions was never talent, or luck, or the particular year of your birth.

It was always only this.

Now you know. The rest is yours.

www.ingramcontent.com/pod-product-compliance
Lightning Source LLC
LaVergne TN
LVHW022102200926
848481LV00003B/1037
* 9 7 9 8 9 0 3 2 9 9 4 7 8 *